The Art of Listening to the Heart

The Art of Listening to the Heart

James Kenyon, D.V.M.

Ooly Booly Press
Chicago, IL
2016

First Printing: 2016

Library of Congress Control Number: 2016921267

ISBN 975-0-578-18816-4

Ooly Booly Press
Chicago, IL, 60640
info@oolyboolypub.com

To Cynthia and our three children, Jennifer, Carolyn, and John

Contents

Iowa: The Land between Two Rivers xi

The Help.. 17

Geez Louise 25

Jane's Ranchette.. 32

ORF 36

The Missing Link.. 40

Love for Professors 46

Just Her Brother.. 50

Lincoln Center 52

"Doc, I've got a Problem"... 56

A Dog's Best Friend 61

Wattla 75

Little Mama.. 80

Those Big Beautiful Eyes.. 85

The Last Days 96

The Hat Lady... 105

Poor Old Blue 109

Dog Gone.. 113

Billy the Dreamer.. 117

Jake and the Shrink 128

Beg'er Pardon.. 133

Honey, Cowboy, and a Spanish Star Fire 146

About the Author.. 157

Acknowledgements

I dedicate this book to my wife Cynthia and our three children Jennifer, Carolyn, and John. We came to Iowa for a job and ended up creating a life and home. Far away from family, we bloomed where we were planted. We each contributed to the veterinary business with a family commitment of helping man and all of God's creatures. Doctoring, reception work, walking dogs, kennel duties, holidays, nights and weekends, and never a disagreeing word about the commitment.

I would like to thank Dr. Judith Harrington, the little city girl, for her encouragement and editing which made this book possible. And to John Kenyon for his cover design and graphics work.

I would like to thank a wonderful community and my animal caring friends for their love and support for these four decades.

Iowa: The Land between Two Rivers

Iowa, oh Iowa. This land between the two great rivers, the Mississippi and the Missouri, is the modern day land of milk and honey. Only a century-and-a-half old as a state, it is in the very middle of America and is blessed with the greatest fertile soil in America. Once, it was the land of tall grass prairies, old one-room schoolhouses, and small vibrant communities in every corner of its reaches: its rolling lands, its wetlands, its Switzerland-like vistas of the Northeast, but always its rich deep fertile and glaciated topsoil in each of its quadrants. Thus was the wonderful line from *Field of Dreams*: "Is this Heaven? No, it's Iowa!"

"All Creatures Great and Small," penned by the renowned veterinarian James Herriot about his homeland of Yorkshire, England, is the quintessential story about man and his animal kingdom. The beautiful language of the farming countrymen is transformed into a descriptive epic of that time and place. The individual tales of the countryside, the brogue wit of its people, and the unique relationships of their animals and life cannot be better told.

To the 21st century veterinarian, this land between two rivers is quite different from that of the Yorkshire, England, of Herriot's day. For the first 100 years of statehood since 1846, Iowa's breathtaking landscape was dotted by farmsteads with barns and silos in every direction. Neighbors helped each other with farming activities. There was at least a one-room schoolhouse for every township. Country churches mainly from the Scandinavian Lutheran influence, as well as the German and French Catholic heritage, brought these rural communities together. Every town had its Midwestern mix of Methodist, Presbyterian, and Baptist churches plus an occasional white pillar Congressional church. These classic clapboard churches were in the busy town square in the larger county seat-centered communities. The German Dutch Reformed were a notable influence across the western half of Iowa.

Wars had their tragic influence on Iowa. Though no battles were ever fought on its soil, Iowa furnished more soldiers per capita for the American Civil War than any other state. With World War I, the war to end all wars, the world became different to these farm boys and their small rural life. "How you going to keep 'em down on the farm after they've seen *Paree?*" was to become their gateway to the larger world.

With the new age of the tractor and the moldboard plow, the large farm family of eight to twelve children started to become a thing of the past. The agricultural manufacturing, packing plants, agronomy, and germ seed industries provided jobs as the mechanized tractor replaced the horse as the beast of burden. The tractor enabled the farmer to cover more acres with much less man power. The farm size became larger, the households smaller, the rural population suffered, and the one-room schools closed.

Education has long been the hallmark of Iowa's heritage. The Palmer method of writing was a technique developed in Cedar Rapids by Austin Palmer. Elementary children across the nation learned by this methodical repetition, and this skill was ingrained in each student. The testing services were established in Iowa; the ACT (Academic College Testing) assessment and the Iowa Test of Basic Skills (ITBS) became the standard tests for evaluation competency of students throughout the nation.

One-third of a century or 33 years after the end of after World War II, I arrived in this fertile place drawn to the area and state because of the animal livestock numbers. Northeast Iowa was the "Garden of Eden" to this young aspiring veterinarian. The mild summer temperatures and timely moisture allowed for corn and soybeans to become the crops of choice to be raised in volume and marketed for food for humans and animals. Shipping and transportation by rail and barge movement down the Mississippi River allowed for a world export of grain. This was a major source of income for the farmer. The transportation industry flourished, and the interstate highway system crisscrossed the state in all directions to share this bounty beyond the state's borders.

Tiling, a process of placing plastic vented tubing of five-inch diameter tile some three feet deep in subterranean drainage systems across the state, made even the best land better. Tiling drained the soil, allowing earlier planting, a longer growing season, and farming of marginal land and pastureland possible. As the tallgrass prairies and pastures diminished and were farmed for grain, the cattle numbers which once grazed these pastures started to dwindle. Fences, which once cordoned off every land parcel, became unnecessary. Many farms had not only the three-to-four strand barbed wire corrals, but the lower twenty inches were often covered with a woven wired mesh to allow grazing by hogs. Such grazing of the fields following the corn harvest by livestock made for ideal food supply and cleaned up the often fallen ears of corn and the corn stalks for forage.

With the tiling and ensuing changes in farming methods, the need for animals to clean the fields started to wane. Earlier planting, earlier harvesting, and fall tilling of these once foraged fall fields became the way of farming. The swine production began its consolidation from a scavenger grain cleanup style to a more confined and specialized mechanized industry. Farrowing or the birthing of pigs in little huts in spring and fall began to disappear. It was replaced by a confinement program which was less labor intensive. This allowed for larger numbers, more environmental control, and better husbandry.

From a landscape of dairy and beef cattle with the forage silos on nearly every farm, the farmstead itself began to metamorphosis. The milk cow that had provided a source of milk, cream, and butter on almost every farm had started to disappear. Not that the need for her products went away, but the intense labor and the need for twice daily milking year-round started to play on the less available manpower. Silos and barns built for storage and shelter were becoming empty. Most were built in the first thirty years of the twentieth century. The sea change in farming, and livestock management was the scene in which I stepped into as I arrived in Iowa in the 1970s. The draft horse was nonexistent except for small regional Amish neighborhoods sprinkled throughout the state. The iron horse of choice was the green John Deere. This state was the home of the tractor manufacturer and some one out of every ten people in the county worked at John Deere facilities in Waterloo, resulting in some 16,000 employees. Another 8,000 worked at the Rath packing plant, a one hundred-year-old animal slaughtering facility founded in the 1880s in Waterloo. Both industries were strongly unionized, and often labor disputes erupted and caused friction and periodic shutdowns of the plants.

How fortunate I was to land in this community. It had a rich Danish heritage, a university, and prided itself for educational excellence. The site of the orphanage dormitory which brought the Civil War's orphans here to this town had been converted into a beautiful college campus with an emphasis on training teachers for the state.

My predecessor, Dr. Lloyd Boxwell, was fortunate to have practiced medicine here since 1940. His quaint little hospital was nestled into an English Tudor style house with a peaceful, shaded courtyard. The entrance to the hospital was covered with ivy shooting up the exterior. The birds were attracted to the flowers and shrubs, and fluttered to the bird feeders and water bath along the walkway to this miniature hospital. With its small examination room and surgery, Dr. Boxwell had a thriving business and faithful clientele who regaled in his kind and interesting veterinary delivery. There was also a capacity to board up to one hundred dogs and cats during the peak seasons of summer vacations and the holidays. Dr. Boxwell was a small man with spirit and a workaholic nature. He had a twinkle of intrigue as he gazed through his wire rimmed glasses. He had once been a stellar athlete and enjoyed many of the local teams as a spectator. His years of serving the country farmers had become legendary. Driving only red station wagons carrying his medicine and surgery equipment, he had a lead foot as he raced through the countryside, speeding his way to make an unbelievable number of farm calls in a twenty-five-mile radius from his veterinary surgery. The ice and muddy back roads played havoc on his automobiles, and fender benders and accidents were not uncommon. The local body shops said they always kept a bucket of red paint on hand as Doc's cars went through more paint than a skyscraper.

He had such a following in his loyal farming community, and his quick temper seemed to make his legend even more unique. He frustrated the other area veterinarians as his prices seemed to never change from his already low 1940s prices. This was always a draw; plus, his unusual treatments seemed to work wonders for the dairy cows, which were his first love. When he said he would be there at a certain time, one could set their clocks to his punctual arrival.

Dr. Boxwell was very suspicious of other veterinarians who might want to buy out his business, and I approached him at a meeting on a rainy Sunday autumn evening with just that inquiry. Originally, I had been working for a very large six-veterinarian practice on the other end of town. Having opened my practice in my garage just months before, I was anxious to meet Doc and see if there was a possibility to purchase from him an office and his clientele. He looked haggard and tired. His wife and office assistant for all of his practice life had been diagnosed with Alzheimer's. His sixty-five years were showing, and it almost seemed impossible that this diminutive thin icon could have run such an active business all by himself. He had many unorthodox treatments that may have seemed to some veterinarian as a hoax, but the farmers loved his spirit and style. A scientist, he read and attended most of the continuing education opportunities at the local association meetings. He was always in church on Sundays with his wife, who had been the daughter of Presbyterian missionaries in India. Doc loved sports, though this certainly seemed outside the character for his arduous work life, which was up to twelve to fourteen hours for six and a half days each week. His son was very athletic and showed no interest in following his father in the veterinary profession. His daughter married an Englishman after the war and moved to England. Though later divorced, she never came back to America. The Boxwells had given their energy to this way of life, and their children had moved away; they just kept the engine and love for caring for animals going together.

As I talked with Dr. Boxwell that night, I was very hopeful that we could come to terms on the purchase of his practice. After I had indicated that I was working out of my garage, he let down some of his resistance. He indicated that when I had first called to make this appointment, he thought I was "an emissary for the corps" or the other large veterinary practice where I had previously worked. As I left, I was hopeful that he would call me soon and offer me an acceptable plan or price.

The fall days and weeks passed, and I had no choice but to make a purchase of an old warehouse building which had no plumbing or heating in its sixty-year-old frame. Renovations started immediately to get into a small corner of the building before winter. Seven weeks later, the lights went on, and the phone was connected, and the small business veterinary clinic was opened. Two weeks after the construction started, I received a call from another veterinarian who told me he had purchased Dr. Boxwell's business but had no interest in all of the large animal country practice. He was willing to sell me the client list, refer all the calls to me, and sell the medicine and equipment inventory for $10,000. I did not hesitate or quibble over the cost and anxiously said, "It's a deal." This proved to be an answered prayer from heaven, as immediately the phone started ringing and I too was busy running at a top speed through the Iowa countryside making farm calls.

In this fortuitous referral of clients came the opportunity to meet them one at a time for their veterinary needs. These farmers loved old Doc, "Boxy," or just "Boxwell," as they called him to me. Some looked suspect on this young chap who had to increase the very, very low prices just to bring in enough income to keep the lights going. With the impending agriculture crisis of the 1980s lurking, interest rates were already at 18%. Inflation was bounding at 13-14% per year. I tried to keep the investment in facilities and practice vehicle as low as possible. My wife, Cynthia, became my receptionist and answered the phone around the clock in addition to caring for our one- and four-year-old daughters. With no money to afford a two way radio, I relied on the farmers to use their phones in the barns to call back to the office to get the new calls and directions as they dotted the day's schedule. In my small pickup, Little Red, I had only the smallest veterinary insert box or mobile clinic. It carried just enough equipment to get me by until I could swing back to the clinic to resupply and head back to the next calls. With these modest and frugal accruements, the tales of this Iowa veterinarian begin.

The Help

"Behind every successful man is a pushy wife and a surprised mother-in-law." This adage was appropriate for this young veterinarian.

But what is a successful man? A good husband? A good father? An honest, upright gentleman? A church man? A good businessman? A community volunteer, leader, or servant? I would love to say if a majority of those questions were to be answered in the affirmative, any mother or mother-in-law would be proud of her son.

Growing up in Kansas, we had numerous African American ladies who helped my mother. They were never called maids or "the help" but just ladies who assisted in cleaning, cooking, and chores. They helped the slaughter and cutting up of chickens. They helped in canning and in shucking corn and cutting it off the cob to be frozen and stored for use throughout the winter. Verna Napue, Juanita Redd, and Leitha Napue were my favorite ladies. I loved all of them and believe that we were the only white family in the area that ever had any such help in the home. My mother was a nurse and was also one of the few women who worked outside the home except for school teacher women.

Verna was my favorite as she was the most regular. She was a heavy woman with an infectious laugh and wonderful smile. Wow, could she cook. Fried chicken will never be the same after her fried chicken. We all sat for our noon meal, which we called dinner. We had other summer farm workers who were often male school teachers. Verna was right there at the table end. My father was able to needle her, and her laugh was a centerpiece of all conversations. Her husband was called Turtle, so named because he was very slow in everything he did, but he could sing with a gorgeous booming deep bass in the First Baptist Church choir in nearby Nicodemus. He worked on road maintenance for the county and farmed a small acreage. When noon came, we were expected to be washed up and ready to sit down for dinner: fried chicken, mashed potatoes, chicken gravy, roasting ears, Jell-O salads and ending with apple, peach, or cherry pies. To ever be scolded by Verna was the worst feeling a young boy would ever endure. It didn't happen often, but she had a profound ability to correct me, and the same act or stunt would not happen again.

Opening and starting a veterinary hospital from scratch takes some blind luck and faith in one's ability. There was only one business class taught in the veterinary curriculum. They recommended that three individuals are the highest priority to any business venture: a lawyer, an accountant, and a banker. Though not in the curriculum, the most important is a supportive spouse. I had all four.

Where do you find good help? Little did I know that so many people want to work in a veterinary office. You know, it's all those puppies and kittens! It is almost as blind thinking as wanting to be a wife or mother. The training for all of these is really on-the-job training.

Cali was our neighbor lady whose daughter was our first teenage baby sitter when we moved to town. What a beautiful name and even more wonderful person and friend she was. Her maiden name was Fornia—you got it, Cali Fornia! Having hatched the idea for starting my own business, purchasing a building, obtaining a loan, finding an accountant, and a lawyer, I needed an office lady. Cali met all of the criteria. She was ever-smiling, a mother whose children were now in school, and was game for striking into an adventurous job that she knew nothing about.

Cali's love and tolerance of people was incredible. She never let any task or annoying client taint her smile or actions. I may need to interject one wee characteristic that really was a hallmark of her personality. Cali was a consummate talker. Wow, could she talk! I had to keep working and did not want to be rude to tell her. I couldn't just listen to her ramble, so I would walk away to the next room as I would shout out, "Keep talking; I'm listening!"

Cali was a woman who could start many projects and have them strewn over the countertops and desks all going at the same time. I really didn't have time to worry about these details. Her people skills were impeccable. What a gift from above she was for my first employee.

A veterinary technician was an obvious second person to be added to "the help." Linda, who had just graduated from a veterinary technician school in Minnesota answered my advertisement in the *American Veterinary Medical Journal*. Innocent and just twenty years old, this little blonde took the job with a startup veterinarian. Her training was a perfect fit for an office with a talker and my wife, the mother of two little girls. They provided some maturity and mothering skills, but Linda knew the science and techniques that made the medicine and surgery functions click.

I had often heard that when looking for an employee, finding a person in another job setting that one could observe is a great way to spot a good one. My experiences were also to find animal-owning clients who I thought were smart, kind, and had infectious personalities.

On a hot late summer afternoon, I was called to the country to see a sheep that was not doing well. The gray gravel rock road had been packed hard from the neighbor's heavy machinery and truck traffic. The dust cloud behind Little Red descended upon the farmstead as I slowed to turn onto the lane. An old barn which was repainted a vivid red with white trim stood out at the end of the paddock. At the gate, I was greeted by a beautiful, petite woman, barely five feet tall. Tears were streaming, mascara was smudged, and her distraught emotions told me this was not a good situation.

Blossom, her bottle-raised lamb, was lying next to the barn. She was dead, but, as is often the case of hopeful denial, Becky wanted me to make sure. With my stethoscope to Blossom's still-warm body, there were no hints of a heartbeat. I had to confirm that yes, she was gone. This only stimulated another round of sobbing and disbelief. Hugging this little cheerleader lady who I had never met before seemed to be the only support that I could offer.

"But why?" she was able to spout out through the reflexive inhaling shudders.

"I'm so sorry, Mrs. Willhite. Many times we really cannot find a cause," I attempted to console her. While still embracing her with my arm around her shoulder, I did a quick survey of the dry lot which had an occasional thistle and pig weed plant that had not been stomped out by the two ponies standing at the fence line. I did notice that the barn had recently been painted and that there may have been a few paint chips from the preparatory scraping still on the ground. At about two feet off the ground were several bare spots where there was no paint at all.

"How about if I take her with me back to the clinic, and I will do a post mortem exam to see what I can find that may have caused such a sudden death?" I offered. When there has been such an unexpected death, the loving animal owner needs a plan that helps them understand just why this could happen. By taking Blossom's body with me, it also alleviated more despair for Becky. I spotted two little girls swinging on a suspended tire hanging from a big maple tree near the house. At least they would not have to help bury Blossom if I took her with me.

I sharpened my knife and methodically opened the body in the same way with every necropsy. First, the chest cavity. The heart and lungs looked perfectly normal and were even still slightly pink. The diaphragm and intestines with the surrounding organs were warm from the direct sun's heat, which had added to the decomposition. The joints and bones were in perfect condition. Isolating the stomach to the side so as not to contaminate any of the other tissues, I made a small stab incision into the stomach wall. There it was! Out poured the gastric juices and tiny chips of paint that Blossom had chewed off the sides of the barn. She had died of lead poisoning.

Not every farm animal has the distinction of having a name. Those that do have a name seem to be more special. Blossom had been one of those. Becky came to work for the clinic a year later. She had been a pre-school teacher. Not only did all of the children love her, but she also had exuding kindness for all creatures great and small. This little cheerleader gave the veterinary clinic the next twenty-five years of that passion for the care of both man and his best friends.

***

An after hour call came; I heard a quivering voice on the phone. She explained that her husband was away at work, but she had just lost a second lamb in two days and that another one was down on its side, paddling.

Could I please come see what was wrong? I got directions for the farm, which was nearly twenty miles away.

Being called to a new farm and not knowing the family brought many thoughts to mind as I traveled the back roads. How did they find our clinic phone number? What kind of people and family are they? What are their livestock numbers, and how is the farm set up? Have they had regular veterinary care in the past? On a business level, it is rather like going on a blind date.

As I left the blacktop and Little Red turned off onto the gravel road, the knee-high corn on both sides of the road silhouetted three farmsteads before reaching the Hull's driveway. It was lined with flowers, and a swing set on the porch was being pumped back and forth with a little boy and girl. A long rope from the huge sycamore tree was suspended down to a flat wooden seat. The bare grassless ground below showed its many hours of use. Oh, for the days when that seat and rope would be twisted around and around then released to spin and unwind as a child would hold on and be given a free dizzying ride.

This was a beautifully manicured farmstead. Two horses could be seen racing the perimeter of the paddock to greet the stranger in the pickup truck. The older whitewashed barn with its gabled roof and high hay mow door bordered the corrals. The chicken house and distant hog barn gave the history that this may have been a century farm. That designation for Iowa was for those farms and farmsteads that dated back one hundred years with the same family ownerships.

From the garden emerged a lady with her colorful bonnet and gloved hands. The beaded perspiration on her tanned arms and face revealed the exposure and toil of maintaining a large yard and garden. She waved, and Little Red came to a stop near the upright water spigot by the barn. I introduced myself, and an internal karma feeling about this farm lady crossed my mind. Janie expressed her appreciation for me coming out so soon. Her two shy children had slid off the porch swing and were now watching this interchange from an elevated tree house next to the garage.

Janie explained that she needed help with their sheep operation. The previous veterinarian they had used had given a shot of penicillin to a sick lamb, and it died the next day. She indicated that her friend from church had recommended that they call me for a second opinion. Second opinions are just that. Knowing that the veterinary care given before would have covered all of the most common diagnoses, it is sometimes easier to dig deeper into the odd things that can be overlooked.

She directed me to the north side of the barn where I found a three-month-old lamb laying on its side, shaking uncontrollably. Saliva and foam was prominent at the angle of the lips. Its eyes seemed fixed and stared into the distance. Its ridged body and stiff, stretched legs gave me the diagnosis instantly. While taking the temperature rectally, I asked, "Have you had any of the lambs castrated or tails docked recently?" Even though I could see the scabbed-over tip of the stubby tail, the line of questioning continued.

"Well, yes, Doc was here about two weeks ago to do that," Janie returned.

"This looks like Tetanus to me, and we need to give them all some serum to see if we can prevent any more from getting this," I confided setting a plan in motion. "As far as this little guy is concerned, it is probably hopeless, but let's try some antitoxin and antibiotics to see if we can save him." I knew that I had never turned one around that had Tetanus signs this far along. I gave him a large dose of antitoxin deep in his back leg muscle.

I explained that Tetanus is caused by a bacteria that is found in the soil and often is also on farmsteads that have horses. Just then, an excited whinny came from the over-spirited horse sprinting along beside us which caught my attention.

Janie yelled, "Maverick cool it. Knock it off, it's alright!"

I stood frozen like Lot's wife looking back at Sodom and Gomorrah for a few seconds before I could speak. Finally choosing my shocked words carefully, I blurted out, "Did you say Maverick?" My face must have given away my worst fear.

"Well, yeah, that's just the name he came with when we bought him last winter," she revealed with an inquisitive expression. "What's wrong, do you think he brought the Tetanus here?"

"Oh, uh, I'm sure the Tetanus was here before that. I just have seen Maverick before on at least two other farms," I confided. I smiled at the thought of this rebel following me around like a curse. Maverick had this thing about vets, and to say it mildly, he was more like a jackass to treat and give preventative vaccines. Having recovered from my initial shock, I assured Janie that this little black and white demon was a long-time friend of mine and winked with a mischievous gleam.

She followed me to the vet truck, and I retrieved the Tetanus toxoid serum and the penicillin to be given to the rest of the flock. Each sheep had to be injected individually. They were corralled, and we crowded them into a small pen. This little farmer's wife was a real tough go-getter. In no time at all, each of the forty-five sheep in the flock had been given their shots. The bleating indignation continued as they ran out the barn door. The sweaty lanolin odor on my coveralls was testament of the contact and rodeo of climbing into the pen and treating each momma and her lambs.

As I washed my syringes and boots, I gave instructions for the follow-up treatments for the downer wether. I assured her that the rest of the flock should be okay and that each year it would be necessary to give the vaccine to the ewes and their lambs to prevent a recurrence.

As I descended the lane, I glanced to see that the children were back on the porch swing and waving goodbye to me. Oh, would the farmer's wife have stories to tell her family and friends! Husbands who work in town don't know all that their partner wives do in their absence. After all, there is the household, the children, garden, yard, and now herding up the sheep and treating them all. How can they understand all of the sweat and dirty little tasks? Then what about this Maverick? Some things just will remain a mystery to spouses.

I called Janie each of the next two days to check up on the sheep. Sure enough, the poor little lamb that was down had succumbed. The rest of the flock, however, was doing well. On the second call, I asked her, "Would you ever consider coming to work for me?" For the next twenty-six years, this little German lady gave her talents to the vet clinic. She was another on-the-job training miracle find as a receptionist, technician, and office manager extraordinaire. Her passion for giving the client the absolute best care and service made her a most valuable player on the team.

Employees, co-workers, and friends like these women would become the foundation for this veterinary team that made the three decades at the Cedar Valley Veterinary Center fly by like the seasons in the year. Cali, Linda, Becky, and Janie—they were the core and established the way for many more like them to bring their best to work every day.

The Help was a book written about the African American maids in Jackson, Mississippi during the 1950s and '60s. It surely didn't depict my experiences as a child but did provide insight and the importance of how beloved help can become to us. It also showed a side of taking advantage of that help that was so prominent of the times in the South. My help was truly family, and each day was a new adventure with now four, five, and eventually fifteen helpers making this team complete. I loved and respected them all for their dedication and work ethic.

Geez Louise

"Geez Louise!" was a phrase that I would utter often for years to tell of my challenge and slight amazement of a particular treatment or case. The phrase, though not unique, for me was generated from my experiences with Dr. Forest and her many creatures. The dusty Pacer hatchback station wagon in the parking lot was the first encounter for my use of this lifelong phrase.

The barnyard smells and even some residual droppings on clothing are sometimes not welcomed in a small clinic room at the hospital. My mustache helped to filter some of these aromas from the farms, but the odors remained intact right there below my nose. I recognized this was not always the most pleasant for others. Rushing in from the country and changing from the blue insulated farm coveralls to a quick shower, I pondered just what could be waiting for me in the exam. Slicking down my hair and donning a hastily wrapped tie and a white doctor coat, I slowly opened the door to meet Dr. Louise Forest and her cat, Edward the Black Prince. Edward was named after an English Prince who lived in 15th century England. He was a royal hero of the time, dying before ever becoming the king.

Dr. Forest (I never could bring myself to call her Louise) was the second woman to get a Ph.D. from Yale in 1948. She was a professor at our local university, and her passions were Shakespeare, Chaucer, and Milton. Thus her myriad pets were named accordingly from some of these literary works.

At one time in the 1960s, she had seven of the top ten Old English Sheepdogs in America. The flash flood of 1960 had washed away her kennels and destroyed her home in the flood plain. Friends had helped her rescue the dogs, and she was able to find a small bungalow in the country some eight miles away from the university where she taught. The fostered twenty sheepdogs were soon brought to this new home and the makeshift kennel which she had engineered.

When sheepdogs get wet with their heavy coats, they become matted. They smell a sweaty dog ripe combined with the poop that they manage to smash as they race back and forth in their elevated wire runs. Their eyes are mostly covered with the heavy bangs that flop over their face, compromising their vision. Fostering these dogs to friends surely must have tested a friendship. I would get to know all of the dogs later in the spring.

Edward was a scrawny tomcat that looked like he had been through the wringer. His hair was soaking wet, and he had diarrhea all over his tail and back end. He was anything but princely looking or smelling. Dr. Forest was so proud of him and commented on how he had been found in her garbage trying to fight off another cat for any remnants of food he could find. She had taken him into her home to nourish back to health and given him Spam and all the milk he could drink. Either milk or Spam could cause profuse diarrhea by themselves, let alone together. Dr. Forest's faded threadbare print dress, brown tilted stocking hat, and galoshes were signs that she had just been outside doing her morning chores. She had Edward cradled in her arms. She had found him lying in the alleyway of the lean-to feed room. Dr. Forest's deep concern for Edward was urgently expressed through her darting eyes and her tanned, weathered, and wrinkled facial features. Never one for much make up, she looked more like a hard working destitute migrant worker than a renowned brilliant lecturer of the classics.

After introducing myself, I probed, "Where has he been and how long has he been this way?"

"Well, he and Marc Anthony were two little kitties that I found in my garbage recently. They are still outside because I have six other cats in the house," Louise offered. "I have been really busy giving semester tests, and he may have been in this condition for a while. I really don't know how long he has been ailing. When I get home at night, it is usually dark, and I have the dog chores and everything. I may have not seen him. I have the two of them that I feed outside, but I really don't know which one is eating all of the food and milk."

"Dr. Forest," I said as I pressed my hand to my forehead, "he's not in good shape."

On examination, I noted fleas and ear mites and an elevated temperature. His eyes were sunk into the orbit, and a faint meow let me know he was conscious but very dehydrated and hypothermic. His rear end and the underside of his tail was badly scalded from the yellowish diarrhea. He was extremely scrawny and emaciated. The rain in the morning had left him even more susceptible to the elements. "Let me keep him today, and I'll clean him up and get rid of the fleas and see if there are any other parasites. We'll get him warmed up and give him some fluids under the skin to start to rehydrate him."

Not hesitating, she accepted this offer and left Edward with the new doctor, saying, "I sure hope you can save him because he's one of my favorites." This phrase would be echoed many times over the next ten years. Her eyes gleamed, and her trust was genuine as I walked her back to the reception desk.

"Cali," I called for the veterinary assistant, "Would you please make sure Dr. Forest gives you her contact information, and would you help her to her car as it's started to rain again?" I would quickly learn that just because she had a phone number, Dr. Forest must have had a phone phobia, as she never answered her phone or ever returned messages that were left with her answering device. Her visits to the veterinary clinic were usually unannounced and very random depending on the crisis at hand. Every episode was filled with drama, yet I loved helping her and the unique circumstances that she presented.

It is incredible how getting rid of parasites and washing an old cat can make them smell better and appear more content and safe. With some proper nourishment even that saddest and weakest little characters' conditions can be reversed. The look in their eyes shows relief and a thankful sense that you have given them hope again. I could see a small smile on Edward's face as he licked the sides of his mouth from the microwaved warmed puréed gruel he had devoured. He started to purr and nestled down under a small pink fuzzy blanket. I mumbled to him, "Edward the Black Prince, you dodged a bullet today. You shine up pretty nicely. Geez Louise, you are now down to eight lives left!"

Edward made roll call the next morning and was anxiously rubbing his thin body against the side of the cage and vocalizing that he was hungry. Upon returning the next day, Dr. Forest could not have been happier. She was effusive with her thankfulness. Edward rubbed continually at her feet, weaving back and forth in a figure eight.

"Oh Edward, did you miss me? You look so beautiful. I have a heat lamp and a nice box ready for you in the barn. That reminds me Doc, do you think I should bring his brother in to see if he is in need of some care too?" she beamed.

"It sure sounds like he could use some cleaning up too. If you would remember to bring him in tomorrow on your way to class, he probably would not have to spend the night," I suggested. I reviewed the treatment plan for Edward, but more importantly, I went over the preventative plan for the other cats in the house. Treating fleas in an infested home is a challenge. Every house is different with the number of animals, the number of rooms, the amount of carpeted areas, and the diligence of the owner. Some believe in overkill. Many do not continue all of the instructions, and the fleas just keep on surviving on the poor animal and even bite the owner. In this case, Louise said that all cats slept with her, and she showed me the bite marks from the fleas on her arms and legs.

"Oh golly, Dr. Forest. We've got to put the kibosh on this flea problem," I said, trying only to imagine the circumstances in her home.

"I can do it, but it won't be easy," she added.

I felt satisfied that I had helped someone in a quandary. I could never quite understand how these cases could get so out of hand or how such bright and capable people could literally not see the forest for the trees!

***

Springtime in Iowa lasts about two days. From the long protracted winter and another six weeks of a chilly, damp, cloudy, and windy time, spring is over in a flash. With the trees leafing out in what seems to be overnight, the heat and humidity start to climb. Months later, returning from my morning country rounds, I spotted the green Pacer that had pulled into the clinic parking spaces. I smiled and had to admit that I couldn't wait to see what the professor had for me this time. I saw her tugging a dog through the back hatchback of the car, knowing that it had to be one of the sheepdogs.

Cali gave me a briefing of the upcoming appointments and the morning telephone requests. Farmers need callbacks so they can plan their time to come to town for various medicines for their herds. Still in my country working jumpsuit, I peeked into the examination room where Dr. Forest and Little John waited for me. What a sight! Beaming with excitement, Dr. Forest jumped up with a rapid fire litany about her students, work, things that had gotten away from her, the rain, the heat, her car, and—oh yes—the dogs. I was greeted with a distinct odor of a wet dog with diarrhea. The pungent smell was coming from a ten-inch diameter wet spot on the top of the tail head. It didn't take but a moment to find the dog was suffering from a moist hot spot. This was a maggot infestation caused initially by matted feces which had drawn flies to the area. The flies land on the area and bite the tissue, leaving behind their eggs which hatch immediately and thrive on the anaerobic inflamed skin. Most people are repulsed by maggots as they wiggle in and out of the wound sight. I had seen them as a boy, attacking cattle that had a recent prolapsed vaginal membrane that had become infected. I assured Dr. Forest that I would need to keep Little John to give a sedative and shave his whole body which was filthy and matted one inch thick all over his body. Once again, treating this one sheepdog was the tip of the iceberg. "How many others do you have?" I hesitantly asked.

"Oh, there are thirteen in total," Louise proudly exclaimed.

"Wow! Well, we need to get them in here, and I'll shave them down one at a time," I said reluctantly and hoped this plan could prevent a further fly strike attack. "Can you bring us one at a time with the worst matted one first, and we will get them shaved down." Over the next three weeks, she would bring in one dog at a time in the little Pacer station wagon with the leash dangling behind through the rear window. The dogs were pushed into the back on a bed of newspapers, sacks, and garbage bags. The disorder and odor never seemed to faze Louise's positive spirit. She was always dressed well for her academic life. If only her peers in the hallowed halls of ivy could know of her other look and life with her animals.

Geez Louise.

Each spring, Dr. Forest would renew this pilgrimage one at time for us to shave down her sheepdogs. It was unbelievable that over these next ten years, they had such minimal health problems. Louise never missed a moment to tell of their distinct bloodlines and how she planned on breeding them to continue their lineage. This never happened through either divine intervention or pure luck that they never jumped the fence to mate with each other. The idea of spaying and neutering such regal friends never crossed either of our lips. Slowly but surely, there started the attrition, and her numbers dwindled to five dogs.

There was limited market locally for Old English puppies. Some prospective people for new puppies always want papers or proof of breeding and registered bloodlines. I have always been dumbfounded by this need of registration when 99% of these new pups would be neutered or spayed and the registration papers would be lost in the years to come.

I often made house calls to help Louise and her menagerie. I was pleased to always find the dogs in a raised cage and run where the droppings would be stomped down through the wire grating. They were clean and happy. The house where Louise and the cats resided was not the same. She was my first experience with a hoarder, and the pathways throughout the house were barely passable. Once I needed to make a phone call while there on one of these house calls. She at first was very hesitant to allow me to step into her back room to use the phone, but convinced of the urgency of the situation, she consented. Wow, was I shocked as the back door opened and, I was immediately confronted by an eighteen-inch stack of piled newspapers, boxes, trash bags, and cases of canned cat food. Standing on this platform of rubbish, I quickly made my call and retreated to my truck to head off to the next call.

Louise could quote Chaucer, Shakespeare, and all of the classics, but for some reason, there was a disconnect between that and orderliness and cleanliness in her life skills. She was an institution at the university where she eventually became an emeritus professor. She was able to keep a cubbyhole office probably a number of years after the department should have asked her to leave. Not teaching but maintaining an office space was a tribute to her many years of eccentric teaching abilities. Reports of this office, desk, and files piled high are notorious.

I continued to be her friend through the conduit of animals. Even as her health and memory waned, her zeal and eyes would dance as she brought back to life the years of showing and breeding these sheep dogs. Though many students and faculty have stories of her literature teachings, I alone know of her love, dedication, and teaching these animals in Shakespearian terms and lessons.

"Doc, I've got a problem!"

Geez Louise!

Jane's Ranchette

On the blacktop and just around a corner from the Millers' was the Zebus farm. This farm was a walk back in time; Jane was an engineer, and her husband, Tom, a talented tool and die maker at the large tractor factory, John Deere. Though Jane had a desk job, she was always decked out in farmer overalls. Her love for animals was far reaching, and her collection of them made Noah look like a hobby farmer. Today's visit was to check a ewe that had suddenly gone off feed. As the little red pickup slid into the driveway, there was Jane in her bib overall Carhartts and stocking hat, waiting for me as she set down her feed buckets. She always had a concerned look on her face, but I was usually able to make her laugh. She often tried to say that each one of her ventures was not cash flowing but concluded that she was really doing most of these animal endeavors for love of them and the outdoors.

Walking into the sheep barn, it was dimly lit with a single hanging fly-speckled light bulb that dangled from the rafter. The welcoming aroma of the alfalfa and the oily lanolin of the wooly ewes in their heavy winter coat with the manure sprinkled straw bedding greeted me to the barn. It would be a scene that would be repeated a hundred times for me. When any stranger comes into the pen, the whole flock of sheep makes a hasty retreat to the furthest corner. Each one of them tries to keep eye contact but all the time working their way deeper into the nervous flock of woolen bodies. Trying to sort a ewe out that had lost her appetite is a contact sport. All

Suffolk sheep look exactly alike. They have a Romanesque black nose and face, erect ears, and a stout looking frame. What a rodeo! Suggesting that Jane could have isolated her ahead of my arrival would have been too obvious, but knowing her Irish dander, discretion was the better part of valor. The bleating and snorting and Jane's laughing came to a halt when she finally pinned her by the throat latch and snared the ewe by grabbing a large handful of wool around the rump. The thermometer is a veterinarian's greatest hearing aid. In the sixty seconds that it is in the puckered anal opening, the interrogating questions begin.

"How long? Only one? Is she laying around or holding back? Has she been salivating? What are the stools like?" I probed. These queries all help in reaching a diagnosis. More important is while listening for these answers, I was always watching the rest of the "nervous nellies" stacking themselves in the corner of the pen. I searched for others who were showing signs in their eyes, even the slight dropping of their heads, or a minor depression in their haunches to indicate they may be off feed also.

"No, I told you that I just noticed her this morning. Didn't your office lady tell you?" she yelled above the noise of the constant bleating and baaing of the thirty other petrified ewes.

"I'm sure she did, but I am just trying to get the whole picture," I apologetically returned.

The examination continued with the auscultation of the heart and lungs. The palpation of the abdomen is done to determine the amount of stomach content or if the rumen is moving. Jane could tell I was grasping at straws as I finally worked my way up to the head and mouth. I slipped my left hand into the ewe's mouth, steadily cradling the neck with my knee. I tried to pry open the stubborn mouth to see if there was anything on the tongue or oral cavity. She was unusually belligerent, but for a sheep, this was standard. This tough little wooly one really didn't want to open her mouth. Finally, I managed to open the locked jaw only to scrape my ring finger on the left hand on the lower incisors. At the time, I was not too happy with her as the teeth had slightly lacerated the top of my third phalanx. Finding nothing in the mouth and no other physical problems, I reached for the doctor's grip that I had set down outside the pen. It had an assortment of instruments, stethoscope, thermometer, foot tools, pumps, and halters as well as medicine bottles containing antibiotics, vitamins, steroids, stimulants, antihistamines, and liniments. With no fever, no obstructions, and no other signs other than not eating, this made this ewe a puzzler. An injection of antibiotics and an appetite stimulant was given in the long muscles of the back leg. The concentrated solution was placed deep in the muscle and not directly toward any nerve or vessel.

"So, what does she have, Doc?" Jane asked knowing that I was perplexed also.

I answered first with a list of negative things that she didn't have. When laying out a plan of treatment, it is always very important to not say too much. In this case, it was easy not to say much because I was stumped too. The response to treatment is important in concluding if the treatment has been helpful or if a different plan should be pursued.

"Jane, I really haven't pinned this one down, but I would like you to isolate her. Could you get her some pelleted feed which would be easier for her to chew? Bed her down, and I will check with you tomorrow evening when you see her after your work day," I directed.

I held the gate as Jane manhandled the ewe rather ungraciously into the narrow alleyway and into a side pen. The ewe bleated her disapproval at being separated from the herd, which echoed back with a chorus of baaing.

"While you're here, Doc" is always the statement and request to look at another problem, usually something more chronic but not an urgent enough crisis to require a call to the office to have the vet out. Sure enough, these come on the days that I am behind schedule. This was one of those days, but Jane countered with "This shouldn't take you long. I want you to see my latest purchase." She led me to a heated room attached to the woodworking shop. There was the tiniest pony I had ever seen. "It's a miniature horse," she proudly blurted.

"Jane, Jane, Jane. Geez o-Pete," was all that I could utter as I held my hand to my forehead in my favorite pressing manner. There are several brain diseases that cattle contract, like, listeriosis, that cause the lining of the brain to become inflamed. This infection and pain causes the cow many times to go to a solid object such as the side of the barn and press their head against it apparently to relieve some of the pain, thus the term "head pressing disease." When holding my hand to my forehead, I often call these "head pressing" situations.

Jane's ranchette or backyard farm always offered opportunities to play "stump the vet." Sometimes they turned into disasters or at least extreme chaotic and climatic experiences. The bobcat in the basement, two wallabies that escaped immediately after unloading from the truck, peacocks, bucket Holstein baby calves, horses, and donkeys were a few of the menagerie. I saw them all and more.

With the hand shape still seeming imprinted on my forehead, I asked what surely must have seemed a ridiculously understated question.

"So, what do you plan on doing with a miniature horse?"

Jane shot back in an incredulous tone, "Well, I'm going to get another one and breed them. Do you know how much they are worth? If I can just have a small herd of these, I can quit my job at Deere's!"

Reproduction! Why do people always want to breed their animals, especially when there is no economical purpose in such events?

"Okay, this will be a challenge, Jane, and I really am excited to see what you come up with for a stallion. I've got to run. Let me know tomorrow about the ewe. Thank you for the call and your business." I slid out of the driveway with thoughts of itty bitty ponies all over the barnyard. I loved Jane and her dreams.

ORF

A veterinarian has many scrapes and scratches that are a hazard of the job. Country vets have their hands in water continually and often have blood on the hands from farm intravenous infusions or surgeries. The blood seems to draw the moisture from the skin and causes the hands and fingers to crack. Coupled with frequent needle pricks, pinched fingers from ropes or stanchions, cattle chutes or farrowing crates, the hands take a beating. Early on in this profession, those scars and scratches are all remembered, and prevention seems futile for future mishaps, regardless of the measures taken. The cat bite, the sharp dog nail slashes across the metacarpals, the scalpel cut into the tip of the finger as it reaches into the cold sterilization pans at the outdoor farm surgery operation—all unavoidable. Latex gloves can help with the water and blood exposure, but those sharp instruments often play havoc with the flesh anyway. Dehorning, castration, and vaccination of cattle are particularly hazardous to one's hands.

As I lay down at night following the long steamy shower, I often salved and medicated these injuries. On this particular night, I noticed a pustule on the left ring finger just above the nail bed. Was this a splinter? It really didn't hurt, but it sure was a different spot that had never occurred before. On the succeeding nights, this pustule became raised and started to turn purple as it started to creep up the finger. Whether it is the "men are from Mars" syndrome or reluctance to ever unduly make one's spouse worry needlessly, I had not wanted to bring this unusual purple finger to

Cynthia's attention, yet Band-Aids could no longer hide the progression, and it could no longer be concealed.

Well, just as I had known and predicted upon the disclosure of this seeping wounded finger, Cynthia went into "code blue syndrome." Not wanting to become infected or further exposed to this malady, I was relegated to the couch to relieve her fears but only after promising to go the doctor the next day for medical help.

With the bandaging and concealment, the next day's rounds, calls, and office visits were handled without alarming anyone of my now throbbing purple exudative digit. Since it was a Friday, I was finally able to call the Medical Associates office to get a 3:00 PM appointment. I preferred to call it "potluck," meaning I would see whichever doctor was able to see me when I could come in for my rare medical crises. Today was no different. This older gray-haired doctor, who was only wanting to finish his career in a low stress general examination type practice, got me for the week's ending consultation. His soft voice and very reserved manner was shocked as I unraveled my bandaged finger.

"Holy cow" seemed to escape his lips as his astonished look immediately led me to know he was baffled by the appearance. It was a cold snowy afternoon when thoughts of only a few more hours leading to a warm fire and a peaceful evening were suddenly interrupted.

Dr. Baker asked me what I thought it was.

"Hey, wait a minute," I smiled, "that's why I'm here—for you to tell me." I told him I was a veterinarian and suggested several infections such as erysipelas, pasteurella, streps, staphs, or even clostridiums.

Dr. Baker's eyes widened, and he quickly rose and demanded, "You stay here and don't touch anything. I will be right back." He jumped spritely from his swivel stool and emerged into the hall, leaving the door slightly cracked open. I overheard him at the nurse's station, talking with someone on the phone.

"I don't know what it is, but can you see him now?" he stammered. The phone clicked, and I could hear him hurrying back up the hallway into the exam room. He seemed somewhat out of breath as he opened the door and blurted, "Can you go immediately to see Dr. Shields who is a dermatologist over in Waterloo? It will take you about fifteen minutes if you hurry." He gave me the directions and again admonished me not to touch anything and get going. As I departed, I tried to stop at the nurse's station to report my departure and to have them bill me. As Dr. Baker caught me pausing there, he again urgently pleaded with me, "Just go. There's no need to worry about the bill today."

I was back out into the late February afternoon. The gray skies and damp air made it seem somewhat gory and even like a Hitchcock setting. I sped away in the little red pickup and was soon sitting in the dermatologist's office for the referral consultation. By this time, I had ratcheted up my concerns about this macabre-looking finger and even wondered about amputation or the inflammation progressing up the arm.

As the doctor arrived, he immediately started his interrogation and history of the subject. I reported that I was a large animal veterinarian and had no recollection of any disease exposure. Within a few minutes, he inquired, "Are there any sheep in your practice?" It was as if the heavens opened and the lights came on as I remembered that about ten days before, I had slid my hand into Jane Zebus's ewe's mouth and received a slight cut on the joint of the finger, though the cut had healed and left no opening after a few days. Dr. Shields stood and said as he retreated out the door, "I'll be right back."

Upon returning with his textbook, he reported that I had ORF, the poxvirus that sheep get. Humans can also get this zoonotic pox when they have open sores or abrasions and are exposed to an infected sheep. He was smiling profusely and said, "If you had been at the university clinics, there would have been two years' worth of medical students parading past me just to see this beautiful purple finger in its glory."

ORF is the sore mouth disease in sheep that causes sores on the mucosal junctions of the mouth and lips. It can be painful enough that the sheep will go off feed for a few days. Once they get the pox, it will give them lifelong immunity. Now, I had inadvertently vaccinated myself for life. ORF or contagious pustular exanthema—what a name for a disease. The mystery was solved, and I could hardly wait to tell my wife so I could get off the couch that night.

The snow had started to flutter down again, and the parking lot lights made a star-like pattern of luminescence. Upon reaching the vet truck, I called the office to have them check with Jane on the outcome of her sheep flock. She happily said several of the other ewes had backed off their feed for a day or two, but she was sure it was because of the moldy hay. I relayed the diagnosis to her over the two-way radio via the phone. She said that may be, but she still thought the moldy hay had more to do with it than any disease. Here I had literally become infected, yet to her, there surely must have been some other cause for the inappetence. This is just one of those hazards of being a veterinarian when the patient cannot speak up for itself, and its stubborn owner cannot be totally convinced that the vet knows much. All's well....

The Missing Link

"Good morning. May I help you?" I greeted the perky, fine featured, dashing lady as she proudly presented herself at the front desk. She was chicly dressed and appeared to be on her way to work. Her streaking black and silver hair was pulled back tightly and held into place with a wide jeweled barrette.

She cocked her head with a punctuated tilt, pursed a smile, and announced unabashedly, "Well, I hope you can. I'd like to watch you do surgery!" This occasional request usually came from an aspiring medical student and was generally predicated by a previous relationship or comfortable layer of familiarity. This was a cold call and started the morning.

I grinned and didn't hesitate. "I would be happy to have you observe surgery. Is there any particular procedure you would like to see?" Still slightly taken off balance by such a request, I wondered just where this lady was coming from. Some surgeons are understandably quite protective of their turf for many reasons. The least of these would be the sterility of the operation, not to mention the anesthesia or the sight of blood paranoia which can overcome even the bravest souls.

"How about a cesarean? I have a Burmese cattery. My vet in Oregon would allow me to assist. Since you are willing to allow me to watch, I want you to be my new veterinarian," she happily added.

That was easy, I thought. The acquisition of a new client was always welcomed, even though this one provided a new twist with a few strings attached.

"Oh, by the way, my name is Kathy Kerr," she stated as she officially offered her hand to shake. She was a university professor with a menagerie of animals. She was not the classic "cat lady," though she did have an addiction and love for anything that moved in the bushes. She taught Eastern European dance, theatre, opera, and choreography. She had a staccato speech delivery, and her intelligence was obvious. Her eyes danced, and she thrilled at her ability to shock and make me turn red and flushed. She had relocated to Iowa, having just received her doctorate in furthering her education at Stanford, Oregon State, and Texas Women's University. Kathy was no dumb head, maybe a little scatter-brained and over stimulated from the academic world, but definitely an interesting and lovely person.

The conversation could have lasted a long time, but as I backed away from our introduction, I asked when she would like to see a surgery.

"Just let me know," she said, as I turned to help a lady with the dog dragging her into the entryway.

Not many days passed, and I noticed on the appointment books, "Kathy Kerr with Orpheus for a physical examination." I still had not heard from her regarding the surgery observation.

I picked up the next chart, and as I opened the next examination room door, I was greeted by a slightly dish-faced black and white tufted cat, Orpheus Negro. There, beaming with enthusiasm, was Kathy Kerr showing off her beautiful, sleek purring friend.

"Oh, what a stunning guy you have here," I greeted her. I was taken aback as I had remembered the Burmese breeding conversation. "I guess I thought he would have been rust colored?" I offered.

"Oh, no, he was my first and came from a garage sale in Oregon where I noticed this little kitten who had an eye swollen shut and an obvious swelling over the bridge of his nose," she quickly recalled. I would learn in no time at all that when asking Kathy a question, I had to be ready for both barrels because there was always a detailed, complicated story to ensue.

"Orpheus Negro is a Portuguese named after the Greek myth of Orpheus who was a poet to the underworld," she proudly reported.

"Unusual," I muttered. "Who would have known?" On numerous occasions, more of Orpheus's background tales would creep into the conversation. He was obviously her favorite. Luckily for all, he was such a gentleman for his examinations. He became a favorite of mine also.

Orpheus shared the house with the Burmese clan of Maucho, the intact "stud of all studs." Then there were the ladies: Birdie, Havoc, and Sweetie. As is the case with many breeders, they give their own vaccinations to their large numbers of cats and kittens. It is easy to learn the technique of inoculation of the vaccine under the skin in the back of the neck for various virus sera combinations. Since there is no need to come to the veterinary surgery for vaccinations, getting to know these animals is more difficult, due to their infrequent visits. One afternoon, following a morning of cattle processing and dairy herd health examinations, I returned to the clinic to see the brown Volvo station wagon with the license plate DANCE, parked in front of the door. As I approached the front desk, I noted a very worried and ashen-faced Kathy. She was quite harried and motioned me into the exam room. I couldn't see any signs of a cat and innocently asked, "What is the problem, as you seem so distressed?"

"I have a terrible problem, Jim. There is something wrong with my kitten!" she pleaded. "I have never seen anything like it before!"

"Okay," I thought aloud, "but how can I help you if you don't have the kitten with you?"

"Oh, I have her with me," as she started from the top of her sweatshirt and tunneled down inside to fish out this wiggling newborn kitten. My shock at the location and presentation of the groping kitten was obvious, and I tried to hide my astonished, reddened face. Kathy was a master of over dramatization and thrilled at tickling my farm boy naiveté.

"Well, let's see her." I immediately noticed the problem as I gently pried her from Kathy's grip. "Oh my, she has a cleft palate and cleft upper lip. Kathy, she can't make it," I struggled to utter.

"I know it. Would you take care of her for me?" She turned with moistened eyes and retreated, leaving me with this wee struggling newborn. It was a kitten from a litter of four, and upon examination of the other three at their six weeks presentations, I heard a swishing heart sound on one of these brown precious darlings. The auscultation of the heart of a one-pound wiggling kitten or a twelve-hundred-pound horse is very similar. I knew it sounded like a ventricular septal defect or a congenital aberration of some sort. Kathy pursed her face and frowned as I conveyed this bad news. Literally thousands of kittens of every imaginable farmyard breeding can be examined and never show such a defect. I suggested the only choice that I could summon—we should give it some time and see if it would change in the ensuing months of growth and development. Kathy remained calm, but I could see the wheels spinning and knew she would pursue information and research all the causes and ultimate future for Olga, as she was to be called. Her Slavic Russian name seemed like a coincidence at the time.

In the coming months, Olga grew normally and was as feisty and rambunctious as any "string chasing" yearling. I listened to her heart every chance I could, but things just didn't change. I did an EKG and referred her for another EKG at a neighboring veterinarian with a newer machine than mine. The report came back the same. Olga never coughed, wheezed, or showed any exercise intolerance—just the crazy swishy heart which earned her a lifetime in a luxurious home with the adult females. She was soon spayed to remove any possibility of passing on the heart defect to her potential offspring either through a planned or accidental mating.

The Kerr cattery conundrum continued as yet a second and third litter of fall kittens revealed more cleft palate defects. This impossible, dreadful condition which caused us to dispose of these gorgeous neonates had to have a solution.

"Kathy," I said as I held my hand to my forehead, "there has to be a reason or a cause!"

Kathy was nearly in tears, feeling guilty that these congenital problems had to be her fault. She felt so ashamed that she may have been mating these beautiful Burmese for her satisfaction and enjoyment and not considering their own physical stress and concerns for their health.

I dejectedly took these latest malformed babies, still damp from their mother's womb, from her grip as she turned away.

"What are you doing tomorrow about 10:00 in the morning?" I asked as I gauged my busy morning schedule. Just a few early farm calls, which meant I would be able to meet her at her home for a mid-morning tea and crumpet.

"Nothing. I don't have any dance classes until the afternoon," she responded with a wondering look on her face.

"Good. I'd like to come by your house to try to solve this case. Have the hot water going for tea. Okay?"

"Sure. That would be great," she said with a hopeful cheerfulness returning to her dejected posture.

The next day I was off and running through the morning country calls when I radioed the office to call Kathy Kerr to let her know that I was on my way.

"KNCR 983 Unit One to base."

These were the call letters, and the answer back was always, "This is base, go ahead." I gave them an update on my morning and got additional calls and callbacks for the farmer's medical needs of the day. The radio was like having another employee as it saved so much time just to set up a schedule and get people called in a timely manner. It saved on my time, but more importantly, helped the animal owners get better and timely service.

Arriving on the driveway covered with a few inches of soft, fluffy powder-like snow, I pondered the epidemiological problem awaiting me. Kathy bounded to the door to greet me. The teapot was whistling, and the olfactory senses welcomed me inside.

"Just let me remove my boots here," I said as I started to dismount.

"Oh, that's not necessary," she innocently said, smiling.

"You don't know where these boots have been this morning," I noted as I used the side of the stair edge to wiggle the high-tops down from my work boot inside.

The tea was welcomed in its unusual, ornate ceramic Chinese mug. I should have known it would come with a unique presentation. I pulled up a chair at the beautifully restored oak kitchen table overlooking the English courtyard. We sat to start the questioning for this baffling congenital problem. First we poured over the breeding program and their bloodlines. Inbreeding was ruled out. We covered nutrition, stress, outside interferences, and the vaccination protocol. That Kathy vaccinated her own cats was common knowledge. I still wanted to go over the frequency and timing. This line of questioning of timing of the vaccinations led me to the question, "And you never vaccinate when the queen is pregnant?"

"No way," Kathy said defensively.

"And you don't ever vaccinate the other cats when there is a pregnant queen in the house?" I continued.

You could have heard a pin drop, and there was a stunned blank stare from Kathy in the silence.

"Eureka! Damn! That's it!" she exploded.

I looked down and sipped my tea and thought of all the unusual circumstances I had seen before, and this just added to the list of oddities. A vaccination with a modified live virus can cause the virus to be shed into the household or environment. The pregnant cat picks up the virus and during the embryonic stage of development, it can cause birth defects such as these cleft palates. Though that class of epidemiology in vet school always seemed so complicated, I had finally been able to solve this case and prevent it from happening again. I even had time for the warm luscious Hungarian strudel before pulling back on the high-top Tingly boots. Kathy gave me a hug and thanked me profusely, and I returned the grateful thank-you for letting me help her and her beautiful cats.

Love for Professors

What is it about professors? To say that many college teachers were unique would be an understatement. Never to deny any of their academic intelligence and abilities, I was often intrigued by their reasoning and approach to their animals. Almost to a number, their animals lived a nearly human life. Each of their own personal lives and background came out in their sharing their animal friends and their experiences with me.

Jack Graham was a tremendously accomplished clarinetist. He had a round-faced seal point Siamese cat named Percy. Jack was always very well dressed in his tweed sport jackets and ascots. He taught music theory, performed in the symphony orchestra, and gave lessons to aspiring music majors. His wire rimmed glasses and ruffled hair made this graying gentleman and his old kitty quite a distinctive couple.

I was touched by Jack's great love for this old friend. Percy was eighteen years old and near the end of his life. His regal movements of his large frame were slowing. Arching his back and purring relentlessly, he would pass back and forth under my hand like this was a massage he had longed for at the vet's.

Jack and I shared our common backgrounds, both of us coming from the neighboring state of Kansas. Though he had been raised as a "city kid," we always had pleasantries to divulge of our once faraway homes. This seemed to be a conduit for expressing his empathy for his friend, Percy, whose kidneys were failing. Seeing Jack in his tuxedo on symphony nights only made his aura and stature rise as a distinguished debonair professor. To connect with Percy on Jack's level gave me a warm feeling of reward and that God had given me this opportunity to help animals and people.

Percy was a cat that loved to take baths. Jack would tell about Percy's unusual habit of jumping into the shower and getting thoroughly soaked while Jack was bathing. If he would take a bath in the tub, Percy would jump up on the back of the rim and look longingly like he couldn't wait to jump in for a swim. He would have done this in a split second if it had been allowed, but he preferred the walk-in shower best. After his shower, he would then leap up on a wing backed wicker chair and onto the vanity counter to be dried off with a hand towel. To top off his grooming, he would sit perfectly still while his beautician dried him with a hair dryer. This routine would continue daily with Jack's schedule dedicated to this incredible feline's bathing anomaly.

Percy, who had kidney failure, started vomiting shortly after the New Year. Many times, there's a surge in cat vomiting after the Christmas season. It seems that some cats just cannot leave the tree ornaments, the tree pine needles, and clear tinsel alone. Most of these can be ingested, however, these small pieces do not show up well on an x-ray. A foreign body needs to be considered as a potential diagnosis when a vomiting cat is presented after the Christmas holiday season. With Percy's kidneys failing, he would have nausea and would also vomit sporadically. He had started vomiting during the fall because his kidneys were not able to excrete the urea nitrogen and creatinine as they filtered the blood in the glomeruli. Since he had never bothered the Christmas tree in previous years, the ingestion of foreign material seemed unlikely. Fluid therapy was started by giving Percy lactated Ringer's solution under the skin. This is a means of making the body absorb more liquid. With this added volume of fluids flowing through the kidneys, the impurities of metabolism can be diluted and excreted in the urine. This subcutaneous fluid therapy was done three times each week for several weeks. It did seem that following the fluids, Percy would appear brighter in his eyes. He was not as dehydrated, and the eyes were not receded into the sockets. He continued to eat but not with much enthusiasm. Some days there would be food in the vomitus, and other days it would just be a yellowish phlegm. His body weight was beginning to fall. Several X-rays were taken, and his abdomen was palpated often but never revealed any obstructions.

"Jack, this just doesn't seem possible that he still wants to eat and have is kidneys failing, too. His breath doesn't smell uremic. I cannot feel anything in the abdomen either. The blood tests indicate that the kidneys are not functioning well. There may be a cancer in the intestinal lining." I shared this with Jack as his forlorn facial expression seemed so hopeful that something could be done for his friend. Percy's condition was showing on Jack's health as well.

"I've been taking him to work with me under my overcoat, and he sleeps in a basket under my desk," he softly admitted. "He is so good, and he just lies there purring, snuggled under my jacket, knowing that it probably is against the rules to have a cat a school," he chuckled.

"No kidding," I laughed, but Jack did not think this was unusual.

"As you know, I would do anything for him, Dr. Kenyon, if there was a chance of him getting better." He looked at me pleadingly.

"I know that, but it is to the point that we need to do a surgical exploratory of his abdomen to either get a biopsy or see grossly if there is any obstruction or strictures anywhere," I offered. "This has been on my mind, but he is so weak, I have not wanted to put him at more risk," I explained.

After showing Jack diagrams of the abdomen and reviewing the x-rays one more time, we scheduled the surgery for the next morning. I gave Jack the instructions of withholding food overnight. When they arrived the next morning, Jack looked even more disheveled. He handed Percy over to me, and I handed Jack a Kleenex box. He said that he had not slept all night and just held Percy and read books to him.

"If you wouldn't mind waiting here in the reception room, I will perform the surgery immediately. We'll have an answer in just a few short minutes," I told Jack. Cali offered him some coffee to help with his fatigue.

I am always amazed that geriatric animals can handle an anesthetic so well. Percy was laid on his back, and his legs were extended to the front and back and tied with surgical ties. The abdomen was prepped and the mask, gown, and surgical pack were opened. Within minutes I had opened the midline of the belly and started through the contents from the front to the back. I did not have to feel long, as I touched an object in the stomach.

Packing off the greater curvature of the stomach, I made a small incision into the mucosa and popped the object out through the opening with ease.

The question of Percy's six weeks of vomiting and debilitating weight loss had been answered. The 1 centimeter-wide, columnar dangly glass piece from a small table lamp had caused all of the problem. It was too big to go through the pylorus and into the intestine. It was too large to come back up when he had vomited. Glass does not show well on an x-ray because it is opaque. The stomach is too far up under the rib cage, and it is nearly impossible to touch it or any foreign body in it with the fingers upon palpation through the body wall.

A few quick sutures were placed in the stomach tissue. I could not wait to tell Jack of the good news. The abdominal wall and skin were sutured, and the anesthetic was turned off. It was in only a few moments before Percy's eyes opened and he was upright. He was wrapped in a warm towel and cradled in my arms. I hurried to the waiting room to hand him over to Jack and showed him the glass piece. Jack gulped and said, "There was a desk lamp that had been knocked over a few months ago. Man, I thought all of the pieces were replaced back on the shield hanging down on the sides." Now the last missing glass piece had been found. With tears running down his face once again, we embraced, squeezing Percy between us with joy.

Percy lived two more years, and sadly, Jack had become ill too and did not live much longer himself. They were a loving pair and gave totally to each other. I smile often when I think of that old Siamese rubbing affectionately on Jack's whiskered face.

Just Her Brother

Mrs. Licuari brought two kittens in for their new kitten exams and first baby vaccinations. Wow, did she need help. First-time pets to a home provide for some wonderful learning experiences. It is not unlike bringing a two-day-old infant home from the hospital. One can read all the books and listen to all of the professionals' advice, but when the front door closes, 'you are on your own!' Some want to do everything right so badly that they panic and don't see the forest through the trees.

"These are a rough and tumble pair," I announced.

"Oh, what do you mean?" she nervously asked as her two young toddlers did chin ups on the exam table. Having babies in strollers, a papoose on a back, or one crawling on the hair-dotted floor add to the chaos of an adventurous visit to the vet.

"Oh, I just mean they are certainly active and full of life," I tried to reassure her that they were very normal but potentially more devilish than average littermates. Toast and Jelly were their names. On subsequent exams and visits, she shared many episodes of their mischievous characteristics and wild antics: the races to the top of the drapes, only to end in confusion on how to get down; one hiding around the corner waiting for its bunkmate to approach, then the springing attack; a great rolling and frolicking game of wrestling with biting and claws extended, holding onto each other; sideways walking up to the mate in a flirting manner only to jump high and run in a "nah-nah-nah-nah, you can't catch me" flight. The next moment, exhausted from the day's activities, they would be cuddled, holding each other in their arms and sleeping in their bed.

Months passed, and I had forgotten the pair when on the table one day was Jelly looking slightly rounded and more subdued than usual. The kids were now crawling all over and distracting my focus from Jelly's belly. Mrs. Licuari seemed distressed as she reported of Jelly's recent weight gain and girth expansion. I palpated her tummy, but the fattened abdomen revealed no particular abnormalities at this time. I weighed her and suggested a re-check appointment for two weeks to see if this weight change was actually a problem. If just overeating and calorie intake were the cause for this paunchy tummy, it could be stopped with a cut back on frequent snacking and the full bowl syndrome.

The weeks flew by, and here again was Jelly. The "tale of the scales" revealed yet more weight gain. Her usual bouncy spirited gait and attitude were subdued. The investigation and interrogation of Mrs. Licuari continued. Questions along the obvious of food intake, lack of interest in exercise, change in family dynamics all led to blind alleys of possibilities.

"She doesn't go outside?" I questioned.

"Oh no," this perplexed lady quickly defended.

"There is no way she could be around a tom cat?" I searched for more clues.

"Oh no. There have never been any other cats. Well, of course, there's her brother," she emphatically commented. She paused. A horrified look spread across her innocent face, as she looked at me. I nodded, biting my lip. "He, he, he wouldn't! Would he?!?"

The mystery of the sudden weight gain was solved. In about five weeks, five meowing little baby Jellies were added to the household. What seems like deep science was upped by the "birds and the bees" outcome.

Lincoln Center

Neighborhoods in rural communities are often united by their country church. Growing up on the Kansas prairies, I had experienced the French Catholics at Damar, the German Catholics at Angelus, and the Dutch Lutherans around Prairie View. Also, where did all of these "saints" come from? There was St. Francis, St. Mary's, St. John, and St. Peter. Clustered in a small radius were the towns such as Paradise, Amy, Vesper, Monument, Gem, Speed, and even a Studley. The German and Russian communities of New Amelo, Liebenthal, Schoenchen, Stuttgart, and Dresden all centered around an edifice of a steepled Roman Catholic or Lutheran church. These were melting pots of nationalities which settled the prairies.

Moving to Iowa, I did not find a single town of "Saint Something" on the map. However, I did find a Lincoln Township neighborhood of Dutch Reformed. The Lincoln Center Reformed Church was the center for social and religious unity for the small rural community. Most of the farmers were related, and all were blessed to be farming some of the richest soil in America. Fertile land with century farms dotted the rolling countryside. Successful livestock operations enabled me to provide veterinary services for many of them. There were numerous hog farmers who farrowed baby pigs in little huts in the fields—other farmers would feed out these pigs for market. Many small cattle feedlots sprinkled throughout the area to utilize the corn and silage much the same way as the preceding generations had done. The cow calving farms existed along the waterway pastures. Sheep grazed on rough grassy acres which were not accessible to the plow. Tiling of this fertile Iowa soil allowed for the drainage of this tight moist Grundy soil. Fences had been removed and the pasture lands drained to become much more productive for raising cash grain crops of corn and soybeans.

Lincoln Center was named for being the center of Lincoln Township in Grundy County. A Dutch Reformed church was built at this site in the 1890s. Its modest architecture of burnt red brick was topped by a white bell tower. These bells brought farmers and neighbors together as a greater extended family. It was a center for social and religious unity. Most of these farmers were related in one way or the other. Learning the genealogical connections required a keen ear and an inquiring mind. Brothers, sisters, cousins, in-laws, and even a few out-laws—this small church fed them all. The intimacy of this congregation and their immense love for one another was shared willingly, helping in farming activities such as planting, harvesting and use of shared equipment. During good times and bad, they helped one another with cattle roundups and pig chores.

Card clubs were a social pastime that religiously brought certain age groups together for fun and fellowship. There were many variations of card games played from pinochle, bridge, pitch, euchre, and five-hundred. What happened at card club didn't always stay at card club. I regularly heard stories while tending a sick calf or pulling baby pigs during a difficult delivery. Farmers were very careful not to call it gossip but insisted it was just a way of sharing information while working together. They never considered that they were being snoopy either. I kept myself out of these entanglements. The saying, "what travels faster that a telegraph? Tell-a-woman!" is an outmoded cliché as "tell-a-farmer" is even faster!

"Did you hear about poor Denny Dodd?" Alan asked as I vaccinated and castrated his pigs.

Shaking my head and not wanting to give any clue that I was interested, I kept drawing more serum into the syringe. I knew from this question that I was ultimately going to hear the rest of the story about poor Denny, whether I was interested or not.

Sure enough, it came. "Well, you know they have the three boys, right?" Alan anxiously informed me.

"Yeah, I do," I nodded. "The oldest is now able to help with the chores and even drives a tractor. Gonna be a big kid like his dad," I offered from my recent work at the Dodd farm.

"You know his wife, Jane, then?" he questioned.

"Yeah, I do," I said, nodding while intently trying to focus each needle injection into the pig and wielding a sharp hooked scalpel blade in the other hand.

"I guess she wants a girl really bad, so the other night at card club, she is telling us of a newfangled method of guaranteeing a girl," he giddily went on.

"Hard to get those guarantees, you know," I mused as we moved to the next pen of piglets. I knew I was going to hear more.

"So here's the kicker. She has Denny on a time schedule. Seems he has to come in mid-morning at an exact time same time every day, and they do their thing. Then there's something 'bout the afternoon too, and maybe even something about the moon they coordinate. Anyway, you know how matter of fact she is?" he asked.

"Al, I just know she makes a great cherry pie. Just had some last week after working their calves," I added, hoping to distract him from any more details. This evasiveness was not going well as I sensed he wanted to share his card club story with someone.

"So the deal is that she tells us all poor Denny's day is getting so interrupted that he's having a hard time getting his chores done!" he chortled.

"No comment," I smiled. Shaking my head, I knew that Mother Nature would have a fifty/fifty chance of succeeding in this reproductive puzzle or card game.

Luck or not, the following summer, a beautiful strawberry blonde baby girl would be christened at the Lincoln Center Reformed Church with all of her brothers sitting on the front row. Arranging the signs of the moon and spreading out the spades, hearts, and clubs would surely be part of the fun conversation at card club for a long time.

Many disease outbreaks would spread like gossip and wildfire due to the concentration of livestock and neighbor-helping-neighbor interchanges from farm to farm around Lincoln Center. Pseudorabies would affect most pig operations. Swine dysentery or "bloody scours" was a continual treat. TGE or "baby pig disease," influenza, swine flu, sore mouth in sheep, and shipping sickness in calves loomed with each new season of the year. Helping farmers cope with building environmental problems from poor air circulation was a continual task. Dick Gerke would have salt poisoning in his hog finisher. The Smiths would have dogs attack and devastate their sheep herd. The Graves would be plagued when the slats collapsed with their pigs drowning in the pits below. The Andersons had a rabid dog. The sleeping sickness outbreak hit the horses at Eicklenbergs'. The sudden death of a mare with her foal at her side at Lupardises'. The death of twelve market-weight steers from grain overload at Larry Circkena's. Corn Country Beef would have two young boys asphyxiate and fall into the silo when they passed out due to nitrogen dioxide gas invisibly emitted from the corn inside.

A great friend and pig farmer, Louis Bakker, once said, "Just as long as we can keep the pneumonia in the barn and out of our house, we'll be able to cope with anything else."

The faint distant morning peal from the church bell gave a call to the countryside with its Sunday beckoning.

"Doc, I've got a Problem"

Farmers are known for their unique way of waving to passing vehicles that they meet on the farm to market roads. Everyone has their own trademark. There's the one thumb up, two thumbs up, one index finger or two, a whole four fingers, and even just a nod of the head up, down, or to the side. It was the same with their own particular was of telling me on the phone that they needed advice or a farm visit. There was "Doc, I've got a problem," "Yeah, I got a problem," "I've got me a cow," and "Nah, this is Russell." Each had their distinct vocabulary. Larry had to have a "goddamn" in every sentence, Brad used a "doggone" to either start every sentence or end it. "I've got a horse." "I got a cow to clean." The rhythms and combinations go on forever.

The January morning brought a frosty, pristine, foggy chime wonderland to the trees. The blacktop to the countryside was a stark contrast to the snow white trees and dormant fields and pasturelands. Dairymen keep their cows in stanchions during the cold and snowy months. This keeps them cleaner and drier and prevents some possibilities of frostbite to their udders. Milk production during these times can increase with more controlled temperatures and individual feeding and care from the dairyman.

This day started with a downer cow at the Millers', a second generation dairy with Holestein-Freisen cows. Upon arrival at the farm, I found Roxie lying quietly in the small maternity pen. Her newborn calf, less than two days old, lied curled up next to her with its large blue eyes and accentuated eyelashes fluttering anxiously as I entered the stall. This farm never had the brightest lighting, and this end of the barn was exceptionally shadowy dark. The pen was in an end stall and was difficult to clean. Therefore, more straw would be piled on top of the older bedding, and the height went upward as the winter lengthened.

The stethoscope from the grip was still cold. I removed it knowing what to expect as I placed it on the left chest of this big mamma. The slow, thready heartbeat revealed that milk fever was the likely cause of her not being able to stand. Her cold ears and head curled around to her side were also signs that she was having postpartum milk fever. This happens post birthing when the blood level of calcium drops due to the starting of milk production. With the birth, the physiologic change and hormonal flip sometimes shifts into overdrive, resulting in a need for calcium to be drained from the body to make milk.

Milk fever is a misnomer as there is no temperature increase. In fact, it's usually the contrary. With low calcium in the blood, the cow becomes placid, weak, and unable to stand. I returned to the milk house to warm two half liter bottles of a calcium, phosphorous, and magnesium solution. The dairyman, John Miller, came through after feeding the nursery calves.

"Good morning. What a beautiful morning out there with the foggy crystals," I remarked.

"Yeah, I suppose...pretty trees" said John.

John was not a man of many words, much like his father. They were no nonsense men who just worked hard and loved their livestock. There had not been much change in their dairy and hog operation for some time. They farrowed sows and fed out the pigs. They had milked a barn full of cows for fifty years. They always fattened out the steers and added the heifer replacements into their herd at two years of age. To have John remark about the beautiful scenery outside was rather unusual.

"Well, I stopped in and found the downer, and I am going to give her some calcium," I offered.

"She was alright last night, but I don't know if Russell milked her out completely or not. I just know she was flat out this morning," he added.

We both went into the small maternity pen, and I put a halter on the cow. Pulling the cows head around to her back leg makes the jugular vein much easier to isolate and insert the infusion needle. There are few dramatic miracles of instant cures, but having a milk fever cow respond to the calcium infusion is one of the most dramatic. There are occasionally those with complications, but Roxie must have known of my tight schedule, and she responded on cue. John and I coaxed a stumbling Roxie to her feet in less than a minute after receiving the calcium. Trembling and muscle twitching slowly gave way to a more stable stance, and she walked out to her place in the stanchion line and put her nose down into the floatation water cup. She drank a long time to quench her overdue thirst. A large dairy cow easily can drink up to five gallons at a time. I happily gave the often repeated instruction for the follow-up treatment.

"John, I just want to make sure you don't completely milk her out for a few days until her body replenishes its calcium balance," I suggested as I put away the IV needle, the simplex, halter, and stethoscope.

"While you are here, would you take a look at this cow?" John asked. This is another common phrase that every veterinarian hears. So much for a time schedule. "She's had her tail up all morning. I think she's due anytime, but things don't seem to be coming along right."

"Sure, I'd be happy to," I returned. Pulling out a plastic sterile obstetrics glove, I inserted it in rectally to see if I could locate a calf underneath in the uterus. My face winced as I frowned, "You indeed have something awry in here." I removed this glove and put on a clean shoulder length OB sleeve and carefully inserted into the soap washed vaginal opening. At about elbow depth, I could not reach the cervical opening. It seemed everything was twisted 180 degrees to the right.

"Geez, John we've got a mess here. It seems she has a twisted uterus. The calf is upside down, and we're not going to get this calf out normally," I informed the anxious dairyman.

I had heard of this in Veterinary College, but this very large cow would offer a challenge. There was one technique of laying the cow on her side and roping a board to her side. Then rolling the cow over to come up against the resistance of the board. Flipping the cow over from one lateral side to the other could allow the uterus to unwind. There was another approach I had remembered reading in a veterinary journal. It required securing the OB chains around the ankles of the fetus, running a rod through the chains, and turning the bar counter clock wise. This idea had to be ruled out because no foot could be touched through the twisted corkscrewed cervical opening.

"Well, John, what would you think of surgery?" I posed as no other options were available. "I believe I could place a local anesthetic in her left flank, make an incision, reach in and rotate the whole calf and uterus. If I can do that, we can get this big calf out the back," I explained as I envisioned the procedure in my mind. "This way there should be minimal chance of infection. We should be able to do it with this old cow standing."

"That makes sense to me. You're the Doc, Doc. Let's go for it," he grinned with anticipation.

A syringe of local anesthetic was drawn. The needle was placed over two of the protruding wings of the lumbar vertebrae. It was walked to the location of the nerve coming from the spinal cord.

"Bingo! I think it hit pay dirt. Her side sure appears numb," as I tested the lateral lumbar fossa with the sharp needle prick. Using the Oster clipper, a wide margin was shaved. This area was surgically prepped, and the eye stinging iodine spray coated the skin generously.

Within a few minutes, the scalpel cut a ten-inch line through the thick cow hide, long enough for me to get both arms in the abdomen. I reached through this small window over the rumen. Touching the calf inside the uterus, I wrapped my hands over the calf's shoulder area and rolled it back toward me a complete 180 degrees. It was remarkably easy to turn. The torque of the twist was like rolling a pig on a barbeque rotisserie. Removing my arms, I quickly placed two rows of sutures, closing the side incision.

By the time I had reentered the birthing canal, the calf's nose and feet were already in the position for delivery. What had seemed like a disaster just a few minutes before now looked like an effortless birthing. The 130-pound bull calf laid on the rubber mat behind its momma. He was oblivious of his precarious introduction to life on the outside. He squinted from the bright lights and snorted the placental liquid out of his nose. The slimy perfect placental membranes that still covered his body had made for a slick slide out the birth canal.

"Wow! That was neat. Sometimes you just gotta do what you gotta do," John smiled stoically.

"Yep, I'm sure it's done many times in cattle country, but having her standing inside away from the elements is a luxury," I happily grinned.

This monstrous calf was already thrashing around and would soon be moved to the maternity pen.

The milk fever cow was chewing her cud with a methodical rhythm. She too seemed oblivious that only a short time ago, she was almost out for the count.

"Say, John, while I'm here do you have anything else you want me to look at?" I quipped. "Two for two isn't bad for a morning's work!"

Mrs. Miller waved from the house motioning me to come to the steps. She handed me a thick slice of bread just fresh from the oven.

"Hey, thanks much. This is special. We just added another mouth for you to feed in the barn too. John will fill you in," I said as I turned to my truck and impending morning calls.

Driving away to the west for the next call, I smiled, thinking of Mother Nature's beauty. The frosted tress were now glistening with the winter's sunlight sparkling through their motionless branches. My coffee steamed from the mug. The Garden of Eden? No, this was Iowa, and I was so blessed to be a country vet in these beautiful rolling hills and valleys.

A Dog's Best Friend

The consuming love for a dog is on a different latitude than for a human being. It is a relationship of reciprocity communicated by deeds, actions, gestures, and vocalization.

Though my hunting skills and interests are limited, I had become great friends with a group of men who yearned to hunt upland game birds. They not only thought they were hunters, but each had a dog that was a great companion and confidant.

Dude Man was conceived on a January morning in northeast Iowa. He was to be a golden retriever, or at least that was according to a phone call I received on a Sunday afternoon to report this event.

"Doc, this is Scott," an excited voice exclaimed. "Sorry to bother you at home, but I wanted you to know, and I need some advice," he anxiously expelled.

"Sure, what's up?" I inquired.

"Well, I have me a dog. It's a golden retriever!" he said.

The golden had become quite popular in recent years and made great family pets. I was happy for Scott and his family. "Well, that's great! So where did you get this dog, and just what kind of advice to you need?" I questioned. I had just been awakened from a nap by the phone ringing.

"Well, I guess I don't exactly have him yet 'cause they just mated last night, but I have put some money down for him. Could I run by to show you the parents' pedigrees to see what you think? I also need to know at what age I should pick him up. I really think I want a male, but maybe a female would be better. What do you think?" His motor seemed to keep on churning nonstop with question after question.

After I had stopped laughing at his excitement, I affirmed that six weeks of age would be a great time to bring a new puppy into a household. As far a pedigree review, I had to say that I could look at it, but I really would not be able to tell him much other than to check to see that there was no inbreeding.

Scott could not have been more appreciative of the information and thanked me profusely and hoped he hadn't bothered me at home. I smiled and assured him that it was no problem and that it was my pleasure to visit with him.

Some six weeks later, I opened the exam room door to see Scott and his six-year-old son, Craig, with this little amber golden puppy. Scott, was a big man with a bubbly laugh, booming voice, and animated features. He was a CEO of a box manufacturing company. He always dressed with a perfectly starched white shirt and slacks to match the colors in his tie. I did not know him when his children were born, but I can only imagine his excitement and joy. I'm certain that the baby's mother would have had to calm down the new father's exuberance, as I was witnessing with this new puppy.

"Well, what do we have here?" as I reached down to see this roly-poly bundle of energy.

"This is Dude," they blurted out simultaneously. "Actually, it's Dude Man," Scott added.

I don't know which one of them had added the "Man" part to Dude's first name, but studying their faces, I think it was a mutual contribution between father and son. Craig was a slight little guy and much more refined in his actions than his father, though the mischievousness twinkle in their eyes revealed the apple had not fallen far from the tree.

"Dude Man, it's great to meet you." I chuckled as he licked my face nervously with uncertainness of the new surroundings. Naming rights are so fun to hear, and I am intrigued by how some names come into being. Such names as Bear, Taffy, Pepper, and Misty are common choices. Dude Man was a new one for me.

Many happy visits and stories of a little boy's growing experiences were shared on ensuing visits to the clinic. When Dude Man was about six months old, Scott stopped by about midday and wanted to visit. I met him in my office. I could see his serious demeanor and the concern that he was about to express. "Are you okay?" I asked hesitantly. "What is the reason for your calling today?"

"Man, Doc, I'm concerned about Dude'" he nervously gestured. "Remember a time or two ago when we had him in, I mentioned that he was growling at Craig when they were just rough housing and playing?"

"Yes, I remember you mentioning that, and as I recall, we talked about several things to try to discourage such behavior." I recounted as I gestured for Scott to have a seat in the cat-clawed Queen Anne chair facing my desk.

On the front of his chair, he leaned forward, and with such concern, stated, "That's right, and we did those. We never go by him when he is eating, and we've cut out the rough housing and wrestling. We've discouraged him from getting up on the furniture, and when we're on walks, he is always at our sides. When we go in the house, he always comes in after us. When we come home in the evenings or after school, we don't make any big deal of it and take some time to go about the routines of turning on the lights and TV before acknowledging him," he reported, slightly out of breath.

"Gosh, that is almost verbatim the more common things I try to have owners do when these dogs' dominance problems arise," I confirmed.

"So okay, I thought there was some improvement, but just last night, Dude was in the hallway, and he wouldn't let Craig by him to get into his room. He started growling like it was his right to control the hallway. Craig hadn't done anything. I yelled at him, and it was almost like something turned on a switch, and he immediately looked at me and ran into his kennel," he finished as the sweat starting to glisten on his furrowed brow.

"Whoa, Scott, this is not good. He is trying to be dominant over something. Craig is the smallest one in your house, and Dude has chosen to act on him."

"I don't think he'd ever bite Craig, but the growl is so threatening," he retorted in conclusion.

"Scott, I wouldn't rule out biting. Let's get him neutered, and I would advise an obedience school to teach him that he is a dog and not to think of himself as the dominant force in the family.

Several weeks after the neutering surgery, Dude Man was sent off to boot camp for a month. This was done in training sessions that included command directives, fetch and run exercises, agility drills, and a praise and reward system for reinforcement. He was drilled in hunting skills and restricted from the niceties of a posh home setting. The nuclear family of a man and spouse and two young children could not have been more remote.

When he returned home, these training directives were reinforced. Over the ensuing months, Scott would visit with me, checking in about Dude's behavior. Whenever any behavior personality problems erupt in a household with a dog, I am careful and very firm in telling the owners of signs and things to watch for and things to avoid. Such cases may involve visiting children, playmates who can trigger a razor thin canine "flight or fight" reaction leading to a dog bite or other serious confrontations.

Through Dude Man's first hunting season, he was tolerant of the other dogs invited to attend the hunt. Scott shared that his instincts in the field were keen, but he was always leery of his anxiety and suspicion of any other hunter. His growl at someone making eye contact was present, and anyone moving quickly triggered his instant anxious attention.

Things during the next year showed mostly a peaceful coexistence with Dude Man at his family home. The playful interaction of a boy and his pal were never displayed. A watchful, careful complacent trust was manifested. With eating, going outside, and an occasional chasing of the ball and return routine became the regular life for him. Never could he be trusted when school mates would be playing as noise and their running alerted these instincts to chase and bite at their heels. After an episode of him breaking the skin after such a thrilling chase and quick bite on the back side of the leg, Dude Man was sentenced to his kennel for confinement whenever any neighbor or visitor was welcomed into the Bittner household.

On a crisp sunny autumn Saturday morning, the big Suburban came rolling into the clinic's lower parking lot. I was watching as Scott slowly emerged from the truck and briefly stared into the distant sky, seeming to grasp for something. He then came striding into the front door. I met him and noted his pursed lips, tightened face, and clenched jaws. He seemed unable to open his quivering mouth as I motioned him into the exam room and shut the door. He started to stammer, holding back his tears.

"It's uh-uh... I know it's uh... We uh," came his trembling attempts to speak.

"It's Dude Man, isn't it?" I was able to help in the interpretation.

"Uh-huh," he blubbered, nodding his head.

"It's time." I too could only muster a few-word sentences as my eyes filled for my grieving friend.

We both knew that the inevitable was going to happen sometime. This time it had been with a fellow hunting buddy who had only wanted to greet Dude. He had bent down and reached into his open door kennel on the back of the truck bed. The ferocious snarl and lurching bite that occurred had to be Dude's last.

I had to be the one that would intervene in this man and his best friend's chapter. Months would pass before Scott and I could meet and not clinch our mouths, looking away and knowing that we each had shared such a tragic experience together.

* * *

Caleb was a 180-pound Rottweiler pal of the college wrestling coach. Caleb and Don frequented the office for their seasonal checkups and preventative measures. He was never on a leash and would stroll through the front door with a confident strutting motion. His huge black body with his panting excitement and shifting weight back and forth would fill the room with his presence. His darting eyes and lateral head movements that cased the room and its surroundings gave the impression that he wanted to help his master through this seemingly unnecessary visit to the doctor.

This mammoth dog had come from an ad in the Sunday *Des Moines Register* newspaper. The Briggses had been looking for puppy, and the wording of the ad jumped out at them. "Farm fresh Rottweiler puppies for sale" was the catch phrase that made Don pick up the phone to call.

"Now just what do you mean that they are farm fresh?" he asked. The character on the other end defined that that these puppies had been raised outside in a barn with the ability to run, play, and move about the farm with freedom—sort of a "free range" environment as urban people like to say. Don jumped into his Cherokee and headed immediately off to western Iowa to adopt the biggest puppy in the litter.

Don had a full stable of tough college wrestlers that he put every ounce of his soul into, molding them to be responsible, respectful, and upstanding young men. This was quite a task for any group of college boys, but wrestlers are another breed of cat and are a keenly focused group of characters. Through his mentoring, leadership, and adroit recruiting skills, Don adopted a band of brothers who helped each other to live up to the high standards that the coach demanded. They would spend countless hours, evenings, and weekends at his home, and with the nurturing of his wife, Dianna, they became their sons and family. Through the years, Don had shared that Caleb had about twenty playmates as these tough guys would wrestle and roll over the carpet and yard and take down and pin Caleb with fun and laughter. Caleb's growl was always much worse than his bite and this rough housing seemed to never tire him out.

When Caleb visited me, he would hop onto the slick stainless exam table. I would slowly pump the foot pedal to the hydraulic mount, elevating him so that he would come eye to eye with me. His nervousness and size would make the table shake and quiver almost in unison with his trembling. Always under his breath and radar was this rumbling, grumbling growl. Don, some forty pounds lighter than Caleb, always seemed in control. He had an ever present grin. His smile seemed to make is eyes narrow, as he rolled his tongue over the snuff tucked under his lower lip. His confident, laid back authority helped me to be brave each encounter. "Don't worry. That's just his way of talking," Don would say as I would watch Caleb's upper lip, lift with its apparent warning of "Don't mess with me," and his peering eyes stared back at me.

Yeah right, my mind was telling me, as I too thought of myself being tough. I was always careful and alert to each beast as they were restrained for my examination and necessary treatments. Whether it was a feisty stallion, a tough horned bull, a protective mamma sow, or even this disgruntled Rottweiler, I always had respect for their warning signals and defensive movements.

Being so tense, Caleb's physical exam was often less than thorough. Listening with the stethoscope was like a submarine with a sonar resonating in the background with the growling overriding any heart or lung noises. Being such a muscular athlete, he would eventually blow out both of his back knee cruciate ligaments. On both occasions, I referred him to a surgeon at Iowa State University Veterinary Hospital. Though only 100 miles away, leaving your best friend and family mate for a surgery or illness at the referral hospital takes a necessary leap of faith. The protocol for the referral hospital is to take a complete patient history including an examination. I subconsciously snickered, knowing that Caleb was giving them his growl the whole time there too. Even with the surgeon and hospital staff assuring Don that Caleb would be fine with them, he admitted that he would be back to visit with Caleb at the end of each day that he had to be hospitalized. It was back and forth the one hundred miles each way once and sometimes twice a day to assure his boy that he was not forgotten and that he needed to listen to the doctor and nurses for their therapy and a quick recovery. Lying on the tiled flooring and whispering into Caleb's ear would make his whole body wiggle. Even as the anesthetic odor still faintly emanated from his breath, he was aware of his friend's voice and presence. All of the hugging and rubbing of his neck and chest seemed to turn on the low growl which was his trade mark. Both surgeries were very successful, but this bond between Caleb and his best friend was the talk of the hospital for some time to come.

These surgeries were the only serious problems in Caleb's fourteen good years. This is almost unheard of in the huge dog breeds as longevity seems to be inversely proportionate to their size. Knowing the day will come but the when or how this fateful experience will occur is a mystery to all.

Rarely ever missing a meal, Caleb always slept on the floor on his cushioned bed right next to Don. After one late evening of entertaining with the last two boys still studying at the kitchen table, Don had noticed that Caleb was not lying down and had been pacing through the family room for most of the night. His head was not uplifted, and a slightly exaggerated drool was hanging and stringing from his lower lip. After sending the two middleweights home and retiring himself, he was awakened by a gentle pawing at his ear on his pillow. This was completely out of the Caleb's normal behavior, and it was as if he was trying to tell his friend that something was not right. "Do you need to go outside?" he whispered as he bounced out of bed to see what was ailing this big body breathing on him. Releasing the wooden dowel security rod in the sliding glass door, Don let Caleb out the opening. He sauntered out onto the grass below the stairs. Immediately with his head lowered, his entire body seemed to thrust and shake. With his eyes closed and this continual rhythmic gyration of his head and neck, he eventually vomited with a phlegmy greenish bile colored pile accumulated at his feet on the grass. A deep groan came as the last of the retching twitches ended. Dragging his front feet with the nails making a soft scratching clicking across the deck, he pulled himself up to a flop down heap and groaned as he laid on his side in a passed out fashion.

The cool night air and the nauseous vomiting having been relieved, he laid in this lateral recumbent position with a heaving groaning manner. Don reached into grab an intricately embroidered Briggs family quilt off of the leather ottoman and covered his fallen comrade. Just allowing him to lay in this coolness seemed to make more sense that dragging him back inside for the rest of the night. Hoping that he would be able to sleep off this acute malady, he himself fetched an Afghan and curled up in the chaise lounge chair adjacent to his pal.

The call came early the next morning. Handing the phone to me, carefully covering the mouth piece, Becky whispered, "It's Briggs, and he sounds troubled."

"Hey Don," I cautiously started. "What's up? This sure is early in the day for you, isn't it?"

"Yep," a soft struggling voice sounded. Clearing his throat and pausing, he was able to mumble, "You need to bring your pink juice."

"I'll be right out," I assured him, knowing that no further questioning was necessary.

The old red vet truck pulled away from the clinic seeming to cough and not really wanting to reach its maximum speed limit. This apparent slowness must have been induced by the driver's own reluctance to descend on a grieving friend and his boy. A lone pheasant scurried across into the waist-high grassy ditch on the other side of the gravel road. The dust flying up behind us made a melancholy sight through the rearview mirror, and indicated an inevitably sad ending was around the corner. Into the long lane driveway, Little Red and I were greeted by two little West Highland terriers. Scooter and Maggie raced and barked along beside us like a greeting party leading us into the house at the end of the tree canopied lane. Turning off the engine, the quietness became deafening as I sat for a moment behind the wheel. The back screen door opened, and Don emerged with a long face. His trademark grin and snuff-thickened lip were gone. His eyes were evidence of a long sleepless night. "I'd like to show you some pictures that I have in the house before you leave," he offered, seeming to want to avoid the morning's sad demise of his friend.

Without saying another thing, he motioned with his head to follow him around the side of the garage to the shaded morning deck. There was Caleb struggling to breathe and in obvious discomfort under the patchwork comforter. "You made the right call, Briggsie," I said with assurance, following my quick surveillance of his pulse and breathing that Caleb was checking–out.

Don extended his own arm out, exposing his inner elbow, and said "I hope you brought enough for me too," implying that putting his friend to sleep was what he wished for himself. Oh, what a bond they had.

Fighting back the lump in my throat and blinking back the lacrimation in my own eyes, I put my arm around his slumping shoulders. I told him I wished that it could be that easy but that I only had enough stuff for one today. "Have you said your goodbyes?" I whispered with my mouth tightened and biting the corner of my lip.

"Let's do it," came a weak response.

Holding off the vein at the elbow, I slowly inserted the beveled needle and watched the blood flow coming back into the syringe of pink solution. With the tourniquet released, the blood tinged concentrate was forced through the venous system. Slowly. Slowly. The steady dripping brought a sudden succession to the breathing and the heartbeat faded to a faint ending.

"Goodbye, old buddy. We'll see you on the other side. You were the best!" I uttered. "Do you want me to help bury him?"

"Nope," Don said, shaking his head and not speaking any more. I knew that no further words were necessary.

I thanked him for sharing his beautiful friend with me for so many years. As he walked me back to the truck, I asked, "How about us looking at those pictures some other time?"

"That would be fine," he softly offered as I turned over the engine and slowly backed out of the driveway. There were Caleb's great mates, the Westies, barking and chasing to lead me out as they turned back at the end of the lane to go back to their grieving family.

Caleb did have a special final resting place. Years later, Don shared that Caleb had been almost human, so he wanted him to be placed at six feet down too. So with a pick and shovel he had dug down into the hard clay soil under an old majestic oak tree. Caleb had his final resting place prepared by his best friend.

***

A free puppy or even better, one given away by a group or organization, is a special experience. Daryl was the raffle winner at the annual Ducks Unlimited mountain oyster feed. Thus, this night when he opened the front door, he bounded in with a most unusual brownish speckled German shorthair looking puppy. He awakened his wife Becky, our veterinary technician at the clinic. Becky had never met an animal or child that she didn't think was the cutest and most dear creature to ever come into her life. Her effusiveness and gushiness was incredible in her love for animals and each one's place in life. Rubbing her eyes and trying to adjust them to the bright light, she tried to focus them on this quiet bundle in Daryl's arms. "Oh my God. What a darling little thing. What is it? Where did it come from? She's so darling!" She kept chattering as she wiggled in her arms to pry the pup away from her husband's sweaty grip.

"Well, you know that drawing at the DU banquet? I could have chosen the new twelve-gauge over and under, but I chose her!" He beamed from ear to ear. Having been married for twenty years and always wanting his own hunting dog, this seemed like a blessing from heaven.

"So what is she?" Becky inquired as she kissed the puppy, and the greeting was returned with welcoming licks. "Oh, her puppy breath is wonderful. It is the most wonderful smell of all!" she said as she skipped around the kitchen like a little kid with excitement.

"They say she is a Drauthaur, which is a German breed. It's something like a special breeding from a Belgian Griffon or something like that and with shorter hair." Daryl tried to remember the description and the pedigree information that he had just learned a few hours before.

The Willhites lived on a forty-acre little farm that they had bought when their two girls were little. His passionate love for the outdoors may have spawned from Becky's father, who he idolized. Anything that could be

70

done outdoors had become his life. Whether it was the restored forest that they had planted, snowmobiling, softball, tennis, hiking, hunting and fishing, all had become part of his persona. His stocky body frame usually looked its best in camouflaged colors, and his distinctive tan hat gave one the impression of a backwoods hunting life.

This was the beginning of a life for Daryl and Jessie as she would soon be called. She quickly became his dog and really only tolerated the rest of the family as she was confined to her back entryway to the house. Her outside doggie door made it possible to always be able to come and go as she pleased. She went with Daryl in his delivery truck as he distributed car parts and automotive products to mechanics and car garages in a seventy-five-mile arc to the northeast of his home. She became very protective of their big rig and made it clear that others were not to set foot inside. She would get out at each stop and lie under the front end of the Ford while they stopped at each garage. Her eyes darted back and forth as she nervously looked from side to side to make sure no one was entering her area. She paced with an unusually stiff, almost goose step Germanic walking stride.

Jessie had a keen instinct for hunting. Her anxious panting and fiery pigmented tongue dripping with saliva were ever present when she and Daryl stepped into a field or started walking a ditch or fence row. Her developed, sleek, athletic body was beautiful in the sunlight. The colors seemed iridescent as sunlight brought out her beautiful distinct colors. When they would head out together, she would weave in and out with her nose always down close to the ground, working back and forth in front of her hunting partner. Often she would halt and look for Daryl's positioning and quickly go about patrolling the smells and sounds in the brushy grass.

In their pickup truck, they would drive together going to town or to Ducks Unlimited events, always sitting closely together with Jessie's head forward right up next to Daryl's like a pair of love struck teenagers. Each with their shaggy hair drooping over their ears, their silhouette from behind made them look like either two Goofies from Disney or possibly just two old hippies. I got to see them often as they would stop by the office occasionally to drop off something for Becky or pick up a special request or errand she had for them. I could really see a worrisome bond developing with Jessie becoming so protective and dependent on Daryl's every movement. His tennis club buddies would teasingly refer to them as "Daryl and his other brother Daryl" after an old Bob Newhart TV sitcom where a sober faced Tom Poston played Daryl and actually had another show character brother, Daryl.

No raccoon was ever safe in her farmyard, but the cats seemed off limits as Jessie respected them and even protected them. Anything else that would move seemed to be a target for her instinctive drive to destroy.

In the spring when Jessie was two years old, a Bambi-like baby deer came to live with the Willhite's. This miniature dotted fellow had been rescued along a road side where his mother had been hit and killed by an automobile. He had been found by accident as a conservationist officer was cleaning up the remains on the blacktop. Knowing that Becky had the ability to foster, feed, and nurture all creatures, he showed up with a cardboard box containing baby Buck. The faith in her instinctive dedication and animal husbandry abilities were well deserved, as Buck lived and grew to be twenty years old. When Buck would run and play, Jessie would chase him. One twilight evening, something startled and spooked him. Buck bolted into the shadowed darkness and ran into a fence with Jessie in hot pursuit. Smashing headlong into the jagged edge of a splintered board, he sliced a deep gash into his pectoral muscles and shoulder. Immediately a call from the wild was heard in the house as Buck, frightened by the crashing accident, was now being assaulted by Jessie. The smell of the wild animal's blood squirting into the air and on the ground was now all over Jessie's face. She overcome by a schizophrenic-like electrical panic that made her want to bite and chew viciously at Buck's open bloody wound. Luckily, Becky had heard the commotion and came running out the screen door to find the two of them struggling as if it were for their lives. She grabbed a broom and raced some fifty yards down along the fence line and eventually physically convinced Jessie to cease and desist. Her verbal admonitions were over shadowed by her distress for her darling Buck. His eyes had turned glassy, and his whimpering murmurs let her know that he needed help immediately. Though being only about one hundred pounds herself, she was able to cradle little Buck in her arms and started for the house. She screamed for her daughter to call the vet and get him here as soon as possible.

Arriving at the scene in about forty-five minutes, I was directed into the kitchen. There were the two of them hunkered down together in the middle of the linoleum kitchen floor. One sobbing and the other cooing. I hardly knew which one I needed to sooth first.

The bleeding had been stopped by pressure from dainty embroidered white kitchen hand towels. I rifled through the medical grip and started cleansing the deep chest wound with peroxide first and then a betadine solution. The cut was clean, but the jagged marks where Jessie had viciously attacked were very uneven and deep. I sutured the edges of the cut down and debrided the bite marks but wanted to leave them open as infection would be expected from a dog's dirty mouth. I couldn't help think only a short time ago in this very kitchen that Jessie was being bounced like a baby with her wonderful puppy breath. I administered some injectable penicillin and told Becky we'd start Buck on some oral medicines that she could pick up at work.

As I packed up my bags and instruments, Daryl's headlights could be seen driving up the gravel road with the trailing dust clouds behind him. I knew that the incident with Jessie attacking their helpless little white tail would crush him. I wanted to alert him before going into the house and seeing the bloody scene.

As in life, it was "not all well the ends well." The following morning, Daryl was waiting for me as I reached the office. He was morose and started telling me of some other incidents of hunting with Jessie. With the smell of wild blood, she was each time becoming berserk and wanting to chew and devour whatever animal they had shot. Daryl was shaking his head. I knew of the thoughts that were going through his mind. His little girls, his wife, Buck, the horses, and even other people that may stop by. I had no answers, only listening and worrying with him. We finally departed with my firm suggestions that Jessie should not be trusted when she was around people and especially when Daryl was not in her presence.

How prophetic these words would be! Only three weeks later, a neighbor farm lady was out power walking in the early autumn morning. The dew was heavy on the grass, and Daryl was methodically loading his truck with supplies for his day's delivery trek. Jessie sat erect beside the car tire with her eyes narrowing and making darting glimpses trying to spot something she heard and smelled. She finally caught sight of this figure coming down the gravel road, throwing her arms wildly in an exaggerated style that aerobic walkers favor. Putting her body in a slunk down prostrate position, Jessie started creeping down the driveway to attack her prey. With slow advancing moves, stopping briefly to refocus on the moving object, she made her way ever closer. Finally at the right moment, she dashed headlong at the farmer's wife. The screaming could be heard like a bullet in the crisp September air. Daryl jumped out of the back end of the truck at the first alarming noise. He bolted at track speed down the uneven rocky driveway screaming "Jessie! Jessie! No! No!" at the top of his lungs. When he reached the dazed and horrified lady sitting there in the dusty road, he could see there was no blood or bite marks. She had fallen and scraped her hands and knees. There was a scrape lesion on her lower calf that was superficial from Jessie's glancing blow of her canine tooth, but the skin was not broken. Jessie was laying down in the ditch, nervously watching, knowing that something had gone terribly wrong. Daryl helped Mrs. Maxwell to her feet and escorted her to the house to put some ice and cold packs on her scrapes. He loaded ,Jessie into his truck to bring her to the office to take care of her. Being Dr. Death once again had made me the friend of last resort.

Several years later, I had taken my friends some six hundred miles to Northwest Kansas to be in a hunting party for pheasants. We stayed annually with my wonderful cousins who graciously accepted us all like kin. We each had our own upstairs bedrooms and downy comforters. Each night was spent reliving some of the same stories that my hosts had heard year after year. Yes, it was none other than Scott, Don, Daryl, and me, patiently listening and nodding as we tried to keep our eyes from dozing off after the long day's drive.

A further bonus of staying with my cousins, Leon and Agnes, was the mid-day dinner, always topped off with homemade apple, peach, and cherry pies. After stuffing ourselves, somehow the conversation came around to Cousin Jim and his vet business. The hometown cousins were always proud to hear of his veterinary life, and most all farmers in my home area had to be part-time farmers and part-time vets themselves. Scott reminisced, "Yeah, Jim killed my dog!"

Whimsically looking around, Don chimed in, "You know what? He killed my dog too!"

Daryl, not to be outdone finished with, "Hey, he killed my dog too!" What an impression to give to my home town cousins! No sympathy for old Dr. Death.

Wattla

At the end of the day in the late autumn, a huge African American gentleman appeared at the front desk with a very somber face. His dour expression was my first of many encounters with W.C. Neuman. This guy was in his late fifties, and his size filled the room. He asked to see the Doc, and was directed to an exam room. I entered and greeted him with a handshake. My tough hand disappeared into his grip like a ball in a catcher's mitt. His solemn, penetrating stare permeated the silence. His vernacular would not have been as easy for me to understand, but I had been raised next to Nicodemus, a town in Western Kansas homesteaded by emancipated slaves from Kentucky in 1877. He sounded like he was from the Deep South. His eyes danced with kindness, and I immediately knew that his character was mischievous and he had a dead pan humor.

"Glad to meet you—is it W.C. they tell me?" I opened.

"Yep, or Willie is fine," he drawled with no enunciation at all. "I got me a dawg. Somethin' wrong. He cain't get up," he softly delivered.

Willie really never offered much history, but when he did talk, it was with short little bursts of words and seemed out of breath, or possibly it was from a respiratory problem. I later learned that he only had one lung, and his deep barreled chest seemed to push out each word like it was coming out of a muffler. His six-foot-two frame was shadowed by his quiet voice.

"Do you have him with you?" I asked knowing that this was going to be one that I needed to see.

"Yeah, out in the truck," he slowly responded.

I followed him out to his truck which had a camper top insert, and he opened the back hatch door. There with his head and neck raised was a reddish middle-sized dog. He looked very alert, but Willie had been right. This dog was down and had no movement in his legs.

"Hi, old feller. What's your name?" I asked as I reach down to pet his head.

"He'd be Wattla," Willie quietly returned.

I really didn't understand the name, but it didn't seem a priority at the time. Surely "Wattla" was not exactly what I had heard?

"He'd be a 'wed' bone," W.C. muttered as I reached under Wattla to try and scoop this flaccid body into my arms. Bracing my knees against the tailgate for balance, and with straw dribbling after us, I made my way into a side door. I laid Wattla down in a large dog run on a recycled comforter.

I hadn't worked on many coon dogs before, and there seemed to be many breed types. I had no idea if this dog was a purebred, but a Red Bone sounded rather official with Wattla being red color and all. I was reluctant to call him Wattla in front of W.C. for fear that I had not correctly deciphered what he had said.

I checked his temperature and all his vitals. I checked his reflexes with a little seldom used rubber mallet like the ones the MDs use on our knees to see them jerk. He really had no movement in his legs. His muscles were limp and seemed dead to my touch. My puzzlement must have shown on my face.

"Ya ain't got no idee, do ya, Doc?" W.C. surmised.

My mind was sifting through all of those lectures in anatomy, neurology, and physiology. One treatise that was pounded into our heads in Medicine lecture by Dr. Samuelson was that you may be baffled by some case, but you still had to surely know more than the owner. This is a nice confidence building idea, but it doesn't always hold water. After asking a few more questions, as I tried to take the best history that I could, I attempted to confidently present my case.

"Well, Willie, given what you've told me about your hunting with him, I believe he has coon dog paralysis." I firmly announced.

"Ne'r heared a that, Doc. Ain't wurf much this way? What happen to him? What be the cause?" he snorted with the wheels of possibilities now spinning through his mind.

"Well, I have to admit, I've never seen it either, but as I recall, it is a type of neurotoxin that they get from a raccoon bite. It progresses up the nerve, slowly paralyzing from the feet then up the legs," I carefully tried to regurgitate some of the medicine lecture from vet school.

"Ain't no good this way. What come of him?" he asked.

"I would suggest that you leave him with me, and I'll get an air mattress for him to lay on, so he doesn't get any pressure sores—we'll rotate him often so this doesn't happen. We'll hand feed him and help him to urinate and have a bowel movement. I can't promise it, but if this neurotoxin doesn't go from his peripheral nerves to his heart or intestinal contractions, there just may be a chance he'll come out of this," I tried to explain. "They say if we give him nourishment and even work his flaccid muscles so they don't completely become atrophied, he may recover. I believe that the nerve sheaths are supposed to start re-myelination in reverse order from the body and back down the legs."

Willie had now become more confident the young Doc just may have a clue. "Ain't gonna cost much, is it Doc?"

"Nah, we'll do the best we can," I said as I stood to reassure him that there was hope for Wattla. I wished him good night. I watched as his big red and white Ford pulled away from the drive.

I hurried to my library to thumb through the reference medical texts and read everything I could find. Rare! Some recover! Reverse order! Be careful of decubital ulcers! Will lose weight regardless of how much they are fed! Express the bladder to prevent urinary tract infection! Massage the muscles! In luck if doesn't progress to the trigeminal, lingual, and facial nerves! May not be able to swallow! Okay, enough already, I got the picture. I was basically on my own to provide good nursing care and encouragement to a "wed bone" whose name I didn't really even know.

For the first week, Wattla got worse. Miraculously, though, his tail reflex remained unaffected and he had not lost the ability to raise his head. He was responsive to our greetings, feedings, and physical therapies. *Roll me over. Pet my sides. Rub down my gastro and back. Flex my knees and hocks.* Finger rolling his biceps and triceps were all answered by a thumping of the tail.

Willie would stop every few days to visit his pal. Their eye contact caused me to melt. Dead pan W.C. would reach in his pocket to offer him a raw hot dog and encourage him. "You be good, do you hear? And do what Doc says, and don' give this pretty nurse here no trouble," he would twinkle as he patted the helpless Wattla.

Wattla was given daily hydrotherapy. I rigged him a sheet with four holes for his legs to let him stay suspended in the tub filled with warm water. He eventually couldn't hold his head, so an inflatable pillow was tied to his collar and wedged under his chin to keep his nose above water. His sad sack eyes flipped from side to side like the paraplegic that he was.

Willie would call to check in on the days he didn't stop in. "How my boy?" Was always his first question. "Keep workin' wid 'em, Doc!"

Not too much pressure. At about day fifteen, Wattla shook his head in the bath water as if he was saying "Hey! Don't get water in my ears!" His ears started to perk up. Within the next day, he was able to move his head back and forth, and it seemed he finally was showing signs that the neurotoxin had met its match.

Slowly but surely, the re-innervation was occurring. Not unlike a baby learning to walk, he was able to first move his front legs with absolutely no control. Then he started to crawl on his belly. He had lost well over a fourth of his body weight. He was very weak. Almost like an elderly person in a walker, he first shuffled, then waddled, and then finally was able to lift and place one foot at a time.

Willie was thrilled, and tears of joy came flooding out of this big man's eyes. "He was always my favorite," he was able to push out with a wheezing voice. "Hear that, Doc? Ol' Rattler will be goin' again soon!"

With a quizzical look I thought of my opening. "Did you say 'Rattler' going again?" trying to imagine the pronunciation I had just heard?

"Yeah, that be his name 'cause when he got a coon treed, his teeth chatta, juz like a rattler snake. You know they rattle." Willie beamed at the thought of his Red Bone coon with his front feet on a tree jumping and rattling.

I few months passed, and I saw a man walking along the highway on a bleak overcast day. From behind, I could see his large frame and the truck that he had just left with the hood up and the blinkers going. I stopped to offer him a ride. Sure enough, it was Willie. He was out of breath and hardly spoke.

We drove to a service station, and I loaned him my gas can. Returning to his truck, I didn't know if he remembered me. We put the gas in the tank, and the truck started right up. It blew blue smoke out of the tail pipe. "Thanks Doc, I be owing you twice, huh?" were the only words exchanged with his eyes glowing with appreciation. He had remembered me after all, and yes, Rattler was as good as new. All his hair and weight had come back. It was rather a melancholy thought though as Willie reported that he was going to put Rattler into retirement. He just didn't want to take any chance with that paralysis stuff and all.

Coon dog paralysis. It was the only case I was to ever see in forty years. This case could not have been published any better in a text book, except maybe the name Rattler and W. C. Neuman should have been in the footnote and reference section.

Little Mama

It was during the dog days of summer on a hot, sticky August afternoon—a great day to be in the clinic avoiding the humidity. I was seeing patients rather than tussling with a cow or horse, swatting flies and me with their tails.

I answered a phone inquiry from our professor friend, Kathy Kerr, fully knowing this would be an interesting conversation. Sure enough, I was not disappointed.

"Jim, I know this is not a normal question, but you always seem to know what to do for my animal kingdom," she rapidly expressed. Was this a set up or what? "Okay, let me start over. It's about Little Mama, you know the one that had her baby raccoons in the window well at your house last month. Every afternoon when she comes to eat at my feeders, she brings her little babies in tow," she rambled.

"Okay," I hesitated to ask more, fully knowing there would be a saga unfolding. I was aware that Kathy provided food for all creatures great and small in her wooded abode.

"Now it's Little Mama, and she has a large lump or mass on her throat!" Yes, I thought to myself, this is a problem that will not just go away. Raccoons are very territorial. Not only will they come back to the same area, but a smorgasbord of peanuts, corn, and seeds seems to draw in all the homeless for miles.

"So, what do you want me to do?" I queried, knowing that I was now on the hook.

"Can't we just give her some antibiotics?" Kathy innocently asked.

"Okay," I muttered. "How about coming in and picking up some liquid Amoxicillin, and you could mix it into some bread dough or mashed potatoes. Then leave it on your deck for her to eat." I had often been involved in working out a treatment plan for wildlife, birds, or turtles.

I had set up the Amoxicillin, and within minutes, Kathy had come to pick them up. She had recently moved to the woods only two houses away from my shaded getaway on the Winter Ridge. I had become accustomed to dropping off medicine or picking up an ailing cat to bring to the office for an examination. I realized that she was fixated on this Little Mama because she had hurried in to get the antibiotics on such a stifling day.

Several times over the next few days, my daughter would be out in our yard and hear, "Little Mama, time for your Amoxicill-in!" being yodeled through the woods in a rhythmic, singing voice. Over and over, I could envision her out on her deck, shaking the bottle of Amoxicillin, standing on her dancing tip toes, beckoning in a pleading voice for the invisible little coon. I remained hopeful but knew there would be more than one possible outcome. First, antibiotics for a draining tract wound given orally are about as effective as a sprinkle in the desert. Second, with food offered on the deck twice daily, this Little Mama was not the only one of Kathy's friends to enjoy the pink-laced treats.

I was not surprised to get another phone call several days later, telling me that the lump had not gone down and if anything, had grown to the size of a tennis ball. "Okay," I again concluded, "we'll need to catch her so that I can examine her to see just what is going on with her."

"Great!" Kathy enthusiastically offered, knowing that I was now on board to help her with the animal kingdom, especially after I had used the word "we'll."

"But just be aware that 'we' are going to catch her and not just me," I said as I looked over the counter to see waiting patients. I suggested it will take a trap. I called Janie, the office manager, on her day off and asked if I sent Kathy out to her farm, could Kathy borrow Janie's live animal trap? Though she lived a good ten miles out in the country, Kathy made a beeline in her rust colored Volvo station wagon to pick up the trap. I gave her instructions on setting up the peanut butter bait and how to prop open the door of the trap.

I had forgotten my promise to help this sickly Little Mamma and was relaxing with the family at the dinner table when the call came from Kathy excitedly saying, "I got her! I got her!"

Cynthia and our two little girls were quickly clued in about the pending adventure. All three were game to tag along to help in any way they could in calming down the "raccoon whisperer." It was dusk and the shadows of the woods required a flashlight. I reached into the veterinary box on Little Red to draw up an anesthetic mixture of ketamine and zylazine in a small plastic syringe.

We set out and walked down the hill and up the long drive way. The mosquitos were out in full force. The girls were giddy for the show. I bit my lip, not knowing exactly how to approach the patient at hand.

We were greeted at the front door by Kathy with the same dancing enthusiasm she had always exhibited. Her rapid-fire talking was interrupted only when she would direct her husband, Tom, to get supplies and towels that I may need to attack the operation at hand.

"She's on the deck out here. Just come on through here, and you can see. I have the light on. I hope there is enough light. She is really mad. I worry about the babies. What are you going to do? Do you think we need to worry about rabies? She is really angry, and what if she gets out of the trap door? Her teeth look really vicious!" Oohing and aahing chatter from the gallery of guests could be heard as we progressed through the family room to the large wooden deck. I surveyed the landscape of birdfeeders, squirrel corn stands, a block of salt for the deer, and empty food bowls scattered in the surrounding dense forest.

By this time, the deck was at standing room only capacity with Tom, a small, pudgy bespeckled musician and college professor; three graduate students who had been practicing their wind ensemble; and several neighbors who surrounded this wire prison frame cage to witness this goofy Little Mama adventure. Great! Not only did I have a distraught animal rescuer and an unhappy creature to deal with, but now I had an audience to watch this rodeo. Like the parting of the seas, I was given room to get close to the snarling and hissing coming from the trap. Sure enough, she had taken the bait and was doing gymnastic moves from one side of the trap to the other. Hanging upside down and reaching between the wire openings with her small little hands. She would have loved to get a piece of me.

I circled the cage trap, waiting for an opening when I quickly reached down and grabbed her tail and secured it out of an opening in the wires. I found a back leg and thrust the needle deep into the gluteal muscles. The anesthetic was inserted, and the circus was underway.

Within a few minutes, Little Mama was out cold. I asked for an extension cord and then shaved this hard tennis ball-sized throat lump under her chin. With two betadine scrubs, an elliptical incision was made, and the mass was carefully separated from the trachea, carotid arteries, and the esophageal muscles. I hadn't noticed, but the crowd of witnesses had all but dissipated. There were no brave souls left peering over my shoulder except for my wife and little girls. It was a clean abscess mass which was well encased so that none of the infection had escaped to re-contaminate the surrounding neck area. With dissolvable sutures in place, I rose from my crouched position to see the crowd had dispersed. Kathy was wide-eyed in amazement and hadn't spoken a word during the whole operation. Wringing her hands with an occasional "Oh my God" were the only noises I had heard. With the sight of blood, Tom had gone back inside and passed out on the leather ottoman. The fleeing students and neighbors were congregated in the kitchen, reliving the field surgery they had just witnessed.

Kathy said this was the most amazing surgery she had ever seen and then immediately started to worry about the babies not having their Mama that night.

"Oh, we'll just put her right back in the cage, wire the door open, and she'll be calling for them in just a few minutes after she wakes up," I assured her. She was laid inside the cage with her head resting on an old soft wash cloth.

"Could I get a bucket of cold water and a brush, and I'll clean this pooled blood off the deck for you?" I asked. As Kathy scurried back to the kitchen for the water, I drew up some penicillin and injected it into this motionless little rascal.

With the cleanup all done, the vet and his family departed to the flashlight journey back through Mosquitoville. These adventures were not often easy to share with the family, but seeing Dad in action on these occasions would always spark great family dinner conversations and laughter for many years. Sons-in-law and grandchildren would hear some ever more exaggerated renditions of the same stories over the years. Hearing of the blood dripping and the odors of the escapades would lead to queasy stomachs, pale faces, and requests to change the subject. The laughter, however, would never cease.

Those Big Beautiful Eyes

I met T.A. Cross on a bright, sunny November morning when I was called to his Jersey dairy farm. The dried golden corn plants stood like statues awaiting their harvest, and black wooly caterpillars were still crossing the warm blacktop roads. Swarms of boxelder bugs concentrated on the south surfaces of all building structures. The leaf piles along the grader ditches were smoldering, and the acrid smoky flavors filled the air. Flying in their V formations, geese were honking and encouraging each other as they stretched their necks and wings in their relentless journey south.

I had long loved the Jersey breed from my boyhood. I had a porcelain collection of miniatures accurate in their art form—porcelain Jersey cows and their calves, the bulls with their small, dished faces, short curved horns, their anatomical features, fragile spindly legs, and rounded potbellied abdomens. They were precious to the eyes of an eight-year-old farm boy. It would be twenty-five years from my childhood affection for these Jerseys before I would treat the real life form. Now with the opportunity to see a seventy-cow herd of Jerseys, I was pumped with anticipation. The adult Jersey cow weighs only about 800 pounds. This, compared to the more popular black and white Holstein-Friesian cow which is almost 1,300 pounds, makes them much easier to handle in a stanchion or any barn setting.

Upon pulling into the driveway of the farm, I was greeted at the vet truck door by T.A.'s son, Tom. Dressed in a black and red heavy flannel shirt, he drawled a "Morning," in a slow nasal tone and introduced himself. This young man in his early twenties informed me that he was college educated and admonished me forthright that he knew most everything that was needed to know about dairying and farming. I really had no problem with this type as I was able to play it to my benefit by probing him with questions for information on everything from husbandry, reproduction, disease, and veterinary medicine.

It was on this late morning that I was introduced to T.A. as he was wielding a pitchfork in the small maternity stall. The freshly cut straw bedding was being picked through for fresh manure so the perfectly formed steaming manure droppings could be removed before they became stomped into the bedding. T.A. was a small stocky man in his sixties and showed little expression on his solemn, rounded, puffy face. His barrel chest swelled under his blue Big Smith overalls which showed soiled wear and perspiration from the hard labor of the daily chores. They had a patch on the knee, and a small spiral note pad and a nub pencil accented the breast pocket. His heavy, thick, and shaggy eyebrows and sagging eyelids gave an appearance of a very tired and weary life. He did not make eye contact often, but his intensely blue eyes reflected the stressful economic times of the 1980s. In a mysterious way, he seemed to convey that everything was not right with his family, his health, or the dairy herd.

"Good morning," I greeted T.A.

"Mornin'," he grunted. "You new?"

"Well, yes. My name is Jim," I explained. "Dr. Boxwell has retired to take care of his wife who is not doing well. You have a cow that is ill?"

"One over there," he motioned with his head. We moved down the long line of cows all stanchioned, having been milked that morning. Each cow turned to observe that a stranger was coming into the alleyway. Their eyes with such distinct eye lashes seemed to peer and wonder why this new person was here. The walls of the red brick tile barn had started their sweating condensation due to the frost from the night before. The steaming chopped corn silage was being forked in front of the eager cows as their necks stretched into the manger in front of them. I noticed a mother Jersey was allowing her calf to nurse with its sucking sounds and tail swishing back and forth rhythmically. This could have been the last meal this spindly legged baby would get from his mother. Baby dairy calves are allowed to nurse directly from their mother's udder for the first few days of their lives to get the colostrum or first milk. This colostrum is rich in antibodies that the baby needs to be absorbed through its intestinal wall to give the calf some immunity for the first few months of its life. The calf is then removed to the nursery where it is taught to drink from a bucket. Some are taught to suck on a nipple bucket but most are encouraged to suckle on the farmers fingers. A small bucket of milk is lifted up as the suckling fingers and calf's head are directed down into the milk encouraging the new born to slurp, eventually learning to swallow the milk.

The racket of the circling mechanical gutter cleaner's clicking vibration made us raise our voices. Crossland Farm had a different twelve-hour schedule than most dairymen. They milked at 10:00 in the morning and 10:00 at night. Their medical calls usually didn't come until late evening and midmorning. My first introduction to T.A. was typical of the years to come. He led me to a cow who was not eating and standing frozen in place. A Jersey's eyes are slightly bulged, and a sense of their pain and discomfort is shown better than other dairy breeds. She stood in a cramped position, rocking back and forth in discomfort, wondering what was about to happen.

"She hasn't eaten for two days," T.A. contributed.

"She have a name?" I wondered, unsure of whether or not the cows here were privvy to titles

"Yup, it's Beauty!" Tom abruptly announced.

"Well, Beauty, let's see what is going on here," I said, pulling my five-inch thermometer from the black handled medical grip. I shook down the mercury and inserted it rectally while pulling the tail aside with my other hand. I waited a long minute while the mercury did its thing. This gave me a moment to evaluate the animal and run through the history with the farmer about the possible causes and symptoms causing the heifer's discomfort.

"Wow, she has a fever," I reported, hoping for a reaction from T.A. I shook down the thermometer and repeated taking the temperature again with the same results the second time. T.A.'s facial reaction did not change. I then finished the examination, starting from her head all the way to the tail, hoping to locate the reason for the fever. "Would you mind turning off the gutter cleaner for a minute?" I asked as I motioned that I needed to use the stethoscope with no outside noise confusing the lung and heart sounds. This sick old girl had normal heart and chest sounds without any hint of respiratory problems. I repositioned the stethoscope onto the side of the abdomen to listen for any movement in the rumen and intestines. Her feed in front of in the manger had not been touched. Proceeding to the back end of the cow, I finally found a hot and very hard udder. Stripping each teat quarter, I located the one which had slightly flocculent or white speckled clots in the milk as I squeezed the teat stream into my other hand and allowed the milk to dribble away. Tom stood in the background, eyeing my every move. If he had seen this recently, he surely gave no indication that he had.

"She has toxic mastitis," I reported, hoping to get some idea if this was a typical problem with the herd or if this was this a new case. Still no help or reaction from either T.A. or his son.

Finally, Tom chimed in. "We've had mastitis before!"

When treating a cow with mastitis, it becomes a management challenge. The cow has to be milked last so that the antibiotics that are given do not contaminate the milk lines, and her milk is discarded until the treatment time and withdrawal time is passed. A Velcro ankle strap is placed around the back leg pastern to alert the one milking that this cow's milk needs to be discarded. The milking machine is switched so the last treated cow's milk is diverted from the large milk tank. I was pleased to see that Crossland used ankle bands or bracelets for their treated cows. If a cow is being treated with antibiotics, it will show in the daily milk produced. If treated milk goes into the milk tank, it will contaminate the whole bulk tank. Should that ever occur, the whole bulk truck full of milk has to be discarded. The bulk truck can hold up to fourteen to fifteen other individual dairies' milk, so the financial calamity can be significant. Therefore, the instructions and dispensing of medications has to be very specific. The goal is to get the infection treated and under control as quickly and thoroughly as possible.

The milk company takes samples of every bulk tank to be analyzed for somatic cells or white cells, which is an indication of mastitis in the herd. Though every cow is screened before hooking up to the automatic milking machine, it takes diligence and a good dairyman to find a hot quarter or slight sign of a tell-tale fleck of mastitis on the testing paddle.

I asked, "How have you treated your mastitis cows in the past?"

"Not had much before," T.A. grunted. "Sometimes treated in the neck, others over-the-top, and sometimes with tubes." He seemed so indifferent and had a very somber look, and he occasionally closed his eyes and shook his head. He had beads of sweat on his forehead, even though the cool barn should not have caused him to be overheated.

I had never heard of "over-the-top" and asked, "What do you mean?" T.A. motioned that you just take a long twelve-inch needle and insert it at the top of the udder and inject deep into the top of the udder with antibiotics. Doc always did this, as it gets the antibiotics into the lymphatic system and reaches to the deep blood supply to carry the antibiotics directly into the udder. I did not want to try this as there was a really high chance that there would be an antibiotic residue in the milk long after the IV treatment or intra-mammary teat infusions would leave. It would not be the last time that I heard of the "over-the-top" method as many of Dr. Boxwell's clients swore by this really unconventional method for administrating antibiotics. I had never read or heard of this procedure, and as it turned out, it would not be the last of Doc's unusual treatments.

A halter was put on Beauty to gently extend her head to the side in order to expose the jugular furrow. A beveled three-inch needle was inserted into the jugular, and a half liter solution of antibiotics was slowly administered into the vein. I cleaned off the teat orifice with an alcohol swab and inserted the mastitis tube into the teat opening. As I arose from my knees to leave, I looked around and noticed there were several other cows in the stanchion line which had become "three titters" which indicated there had been previous mastitis problems. When mastitis is not detected early enough and treated aggressively, the whole quarter of the udder can be lost, wither or shrink down. The quarter may also become enlarged and very hard with scar tissue.

"I'll be back tomorrow to give her another IV. I would like for you to use these antibiotic tubes for the next three days. Use them in all four quarters to see if hitting this quickly controls this infection," I directed Tom.

"Doc never did it this way," T.A. replied finally, realizing that this was a different method.

"Well, let's just give this a try anyway, and I'll see you tomorrow morning about this time."

Tom asked again for the instructions as he juggled the tubes nonchalantly. I had the feeling that this was one of those cases that had been going on too long. No matter how hard and aggressive we were with any treatment, this quarter may be lost.

As I cleaned the IV set in the parlor, I noticed T.A.'s wife cleaning up the morning milking machines. She had some characteristics that suggested a long struggle with some health problems. Helping Mrs. Cross was another son who appeared to have some handicap. I hurried back to my pickup to continue the rest of my calls for the day. I washed my boots in disinfectant with the remaining water in my bucket. The bucket was dried and replaced it in its slot in the vet truck. Tom escorted me back to the driveway and wanted to show that he had a handle on things. It is always a fine line between being in too much of a hurry or being so slow that the farmer perceives you are not busy and can just languish in lengthy visiting. As I learned, Tom would always have time to talk; unfortunately this often occurred when he should have been working and staying ahead of the myriad jobs that make for a successfully managed dairy.

"I don't have much hope for that cow," Tom emphatically droned. "These tubes never worked in the past."

"Gosh, I hope these are a different antibiotic and that the combination of the IV and tubes will do the trick," I tried to give the best scenario.

"You probably should have treated her over-the-top!" He begrudgingly muttered.

"We should see some improvement by tomorrow. Let's give it a day to see if we can knock this bug," I tried to sound confident. "Drink coffee?" I asked as I reached for my thermos, pouring myself a mug full before heading off for the next call.

"Never touch the stuff," Tom quickly snipped. It was apparent that I would need to have a few successful treatments before he would accept this new doctor. I bid him good afternoon and stepped on the gas pedal.

I followed up the next morning at Crossland as I scurried around the countryside. The sweet dusty smell of the wind blowing across the recently harvested corn stalks filled the air. Mr. Cross was coming out of the barn as I rolled to a stop. He had on the same shirt and overalls as the day before. A whisp of grizzled hair poked out from under his cap. He tipped his cap to greet me.

"I fancy you're here to have another look at the heifer. Well, young lad, happy to tell ya she's doing quite well. Eating everything and anything put in front of her," T.A. happily reported. "I think ya may be onto something good here. It's about time."

"Man, that's great to hear. I know with so many cows coming through that parlor, it's a chore to watch everything. If you don't mind, I would like check her over and give her another IV—I won't be a nuisance. It sounds like we're heading the right way." I smiled and tipped my hat to him in return.

"No problem, young chap," T.A. happily nodded as he turned to saunter back to his work.

This was a great start in helping this dairy cow. Several calls each month would keep me coming back to Crossland. During the 1980s, the farm crisis plagued most small farming operations. The sins of government intervention in agriculture had caused a catastrophic combination of conditions. The soil bank or land set aside programs of the 1950s, which had taken marginal land out of production, was again plowed under to plant fence row to fence row. Over-production of grain ensued. Commodity prices went in the tank and depressed the market. Our Russian cousins, thinking they could manage Afghanistan, invaded, causing the American grain embargo. Grain sales stopped overnight. No area was in more distress than small dairies.

I had sensed correctly that the Crosses were stressed and had deep concerns that there was trouble looming for them. With the son, Tom, and his family returning to the operation, there was not enough income to support two families. The term "prosperous farmer" was certainly a misnomer. By this time, I was being called to thirty-one small dairy herds. The banks were pulling back credit for any additional financing. Interest rates soared to double digits, then to 15% and even reached 20% in some areas for short-term money financing. It became impossible to produce enough milk at these prices to make ends meet. There is no group with more pride than farmers, and this economic strain was pulling across the heartland like cobwebs in the wind. Much like a series of cascading waterfalls, it kept coming with no end in sight.

Mr. T.A. Cross became a regular at the front desk of the veterinary clinic. He would stop in to pay his bill with a perfectly penned bank check.

He seemed to yearn for someone to visit with. His eyes showed strain, though he seemed uplifted as Cali would offer him coffee and light conversation. The corners of his lips would turn up, and a pleasant expression would replace the hopeless, forlorn look on his face. If ever there was a man who needed a friend to talk things over with, this was him.

Over the next summer, a drought had worsened life at Crossland. The corn withered and dried before it was even shoulder high. The alfalfa for making hay was stunted and stopped growing. Its lush green carpet with lavender flowers shriveled from lack of rain. Mr. Cross had to tell his son there was no hope to continue to pay him a salary to stay and help any longer. Still, milking so many cows twice daily with his troubled wife and handicapped son continued.

At times, I got the feeling that my regular calls for various cases were also therapy for an ailing Mr. Cross as he slipped further into the chasms of debt.

Through it all these dear little Jerseys kept producing milk. The herd health was actually improving as our conversations and changes in daily management had reduced some of the lingering disease outbreaks, but how much can a man do to turn around a sinking ship?

It was on a noontime farm call that this proud man confided in me. The bank was forcing him out of business. He would have to sell his cows that had been in the family for over forty years. The architecturally unique, tiled barn would no longer have a caretaker. The maternity pen, the stanchions, the silo, the manger, and even the gutter cleaner would all be quieted and would cease to have any use. The mammoth milk tank and immaculately designed and clean milking parlor would sit idle from their decades of twice daily use.

How and where would the cows go? What about T.A. and his troubled family? Does a man of his age get another job? Where could the family move? The sturdy brick home that his family had built and lived in for over forty years would be abandoned. These questions spun around in my mind.

A tear rolled down his dusty cheek as he stood by the cow's rump, holding the tail aside. I placed some uterine pessaries deep inside the uterus of this dainty young cow to treat infection. "How can I help you get things ready for the dispersal?" was my only response to this impending news.

"Well, I want to have a sale here on the farm. I have all the pedigrees and registration papers on every animal. Records of every breeding and individual production numbers and everything," T.A. continued. "My father had established this herd and after the war left it to me to carry on," he lamented. "Now all of these beautiful cows will be scattered hither and yon, never to see each other again," he continued. "Oh, to add to this dilemma, the doctors have given me four months to live," he somberly added.

I choked, astonished, and said, "Dang, T.A.! Job couldn't have had so much thrown at him!" I sadly concluded, "Can Tom come home to help us get them ready?"

"Well, ya know, he's got a job in Michigan. Just have to see," he pondered.

A plan for blood testing each animal was drawn up. Individual health papers for every cow and calf were made with cross matching of pedigrees and tattoos. A date for the November sale was chosen. The auctioneer met to make suggestions for the advertising and helped design the sale ring with metal gates. Straw bales would be used around the outside of the arena for seating. T.A.'s health continued to fail. He moved slower with each ensuing day.

A midnight call came at my bedside. "Doc, I've got a problem. She didn't come up...really a big belly...due date....tail hanging out. She's Daisy May's calf, Molly May...she's in trouble," came the short quick sentences over the receiver.

"I'll be right out. Do you have a good flashlight?" I asked as I was already pulling myself out of bed. Time was of the essence as there is no way to know how long the cow had been in labor. A delivery with only the tail out it is never a good sign.

The headlights marked the way over the frost covered pasture. Small glaciated stones and hard "cow pies" made the way look like an obstacle course as the lights bumped up and down in the crisp night air.

"She's over there," T.A. pointed with his flashlight from the passenger seat.

"Holy cow! Now I see her. Is she still alive?" I muttered as we approached her side. There was still steam coming from her dry, mucous-caked nostrils. She was lying prostrate on her side with all four of her legs straight out horizontally. Her huge bloated abdomen gave the look of an over inflated balloon. This little heifer had to be feeling miserable.

I quickly drew some hot water from the vet box reservoir. I grabbed the OB chains, the calf jack, some lubricant, and a syringe of local anesthetic to numb the back end of the heifer. I injected the lidocaine into the epidural space and proceeded to clean the vaginal area with some iodine soapy scrub. The tail was obviously the only thing that was protruding from her birthing canal. The calf would likely be dead, I thought. Now that she was numbed and not straining, my hope was that we could just save Molly. I took off my shirt and stripped to the waist. Lying on the frosty ground, I slowly pushed the calf's rump and tail forward in the pelvis with a strong steady motion. "Where were the back legs?" I worried. At last, the little bugger dropped to the brim of the pelvis. There wasn't much room to work as the long stay there had caused damage to the swollen birth canal. Reaching deep inside of this cavernous darkness, I touched a back hoof. With my eyes closed, it did not matter that the dim flashlight was the only external light available. With one hand pushing the rump and the other cradling the hoof, the foot came up and backwards. The other foot was found up under the calf's tummy and extracted backwards. Finally, with both back feet out, the OB chains were applied to the feet, and the calf was ready to be pulled. With a grunt and rhythmic straining, Molly helped push this newborn out of its wedged position. The calf's slimy placenta covered its face, and though peeled back of its nose, there was no breath. In the dim light I could see the heart thumping regularly. Still no breath. I retreated to the vet box and drew up a milliliter of Dopram and injected it into the tongue. I grabbed the neonate's face and placed my whole mouth over its mouth and nostril, blowing hard as I watched the chest expand. After a half dozen forced breaths from my CPR, this fragile little calf puffed one breath on its own. Then a second and a third followed. The CPR and the Dopram had done the trick.

I washed and sterilized my arms and hands and reentered the heifer's womb. I was surprised to touch a nose. Then two front feet. After a good contraction, out came calf number two. This one was much more alive. I grabbed its back legs and swung this little bundle upside down. The placental fluids and mucous ran out of its nose and mouth. Satisfied that these twins were going to make it, I cleaned up my arm again to place some antibiotic boluses in the womb to fight against any possible infection.

"Oh my gosh!" I shouted as my voice carried in the stillness of the night. "By gum, there's another one in there," I smiled with excitement. This one was even feistier than number two. I went through the same procedure of swinging it upside down to clear the lungs.

By this time, number one and two were struggling to get to their feet. Watching them first up on their haunches with their rear ends in the air was like watching Bambi on an ice covered pond.

I raised each of their back legs to check their sexes. I shouted, "T.A. you're not gonna believe this. They're all girls. Yep, all of them are heifers. Can you believe that?" Only in cattle is it important that the twin not be a male because the coupling heifer calf, called a Freemartin, will be sterile.

"Holy cow! These little girls will pass on their genetics three times," he choked and sobbed into his handkerchief. The moon had come out from under the clouds and cast long shadows as we cleaned up the equipment. This harvest moon in its brilliance made up for the battery as the flashlight had seen its final minutes.

Molly had sat up and had started licking her new family. Calf number three had worked her way up to the front and was nuzzling her momma, looking for a faucet of milk. I lifted all three of them into the warm cab of the pickup truck. T.A. drove the pickup as the new warm little bodies steamed over the wind shield. I followed Molly, walking behind her. She had no intentions of letting the triplets get out of her sight. The maternity pen with its golden, knee-deep oat straw was a comfortable ending for this new mother and her crew.

"This is really a perfect night. I can't think of a better way to cap off my life," Mr. Cross said, holding himself with immense pain up on the metal gate.

I squeezed his arm as I closed the gate. "Thank you for sharing it and allowing me to be part of that life too," I parted with a hugging arm around his shoulder.

Later, Molly was led into the sale ring. She had been washed and groomed. "That'll be five hundred. Now who'll give me six—now seven— seven-fifty—now eight? Come on! Are you still with me? Yes! Now nine— ten—and it's back to you for ten-fifty? Ten-fifty? Yes! Now eleven. Eleven once? Eleven twice? Sold to number thirty-eight! This man here in the brown hat for ten-fifty!"

The Last Days

Gerri! Imagine the hand to the forehead stance or head pressing disease! This wonderful woman challenged the bridge from communication to reality. How can I describe these experiences without telling of Geraldine? She was born a twin to a brother named Gerald. Gerald and Geraldine. Really? Rather unique from their birth names, she was a professor at the university where she taught leadership. An incredibly bright lady, she daily read *The New York Times* and clipped articles for my reading. She was a "green" advocate in all of her personal activities from plants to the environment. She was a social advocate, and her political beliefs were just a little left of center. She could talk issues and world events with great understanding and analysis, and she deeply loved all creatures.

Gerri always dressed nicely and her favorite colors were black and orange. Her dark eye liner distinguished her black and silver hair and complimented her makeup. Oh, and occasionally there was a green or red dyed strip of hair just for a change. She was always on the go with lectures, continuing education meetings, and planning leadership forums. She was unquestionably talented with her work life. Having been married for a short time, she reported it did not work out between the academic and one from the "outside world." She would lament that she still loved him and communicated with him often. I always wondered what a unique character he must have been and about the details but did not think it pertinent to our frequent relations with her flock of characters.

We first met with a dog named Orpheus or Orphy for short. How could it be that two of my very interesting lady profs could have an animal named Orpheus? That Greek myth god or royalty from the underground sure left his mark here with my lady professors. Orphy was a mid-sized crossbred black lab and a notorious crotch sniffer. I know this may sound crude, but to not mention this about him would be a discredit to his character. This always meant that when he would approach another person, he would head for you-know-where. I would automatically take the "lotus leaf" position. By turning sideways quickly, this kept me from getting the moist nose plant touch of his habitual greeting. Graying in the muzzle, he always had a slightly tilted head like he understood everything you were saying about him. As often happens with these lab types, he had numerous fatty lumps under the skin surface. These were benign deposits of adipose tissue. They were harmless but always made Orphy appear slightly awry and out of kilter. The cause is unknown, but some breeds are more predisposed. He was always dancing and on the move even while on the leash. Gerri's wonderful laugh and her smile were at their finest when she arrived at the veterinary office with Orphy in tow. He would encircle her, going around and around like a top, causing a tripping, panicked scene. Gerri would keep chuckling as though this were neat behavior. Often, she would get off balance and call for assistance. I would lend a hand at trying to help in untangling the leash wrapped many times around her legs, always remembering to keep myself covered from a quick sneak nose attack. It would have been a home movie hit production.

At home, Orphy had to share Gerri's love with Virginia, a flabby-faced, overweight Shar Pei with wrinkles everywhere. Virginia had a scarred white eye and always looked like a brawler. They both tolerated Jake, an ancient rescued terrier Gerri had saved from death row at the local shelter. He was scrawny and almost blind and would bite if restrained to hold or move him into a cage. What a threesome! This trifecta would often board with us while Gerri was away lecturing or at continuing education events. Their personalities each became known, and one could not say the name of one without having to consider all three. Orphy, Virginia, and Jake! Orphy, Virginia, and Jake! The calamity when they rolled in for an overnight stay was a scene for all times. As they tumbled out of the van on leashes of varying lengths, spinning, half-choking, tangled, through the legs and always snorting, looking for the office cat, Patches, and of course, the laughing professor. The sniffer, the brawler, and the biter. Their diets, medical issues, medications, special blankets, and shortcomings had to be considered along with their individual medical plans. They came with their own special bags filled with rawhides, pacifiers, and stuffed toys. Gerri also included makeshift contraptions that she made to attach to the cages—each one with a name on it, Orphy, Virginia, Jake! These contraptions, recycled boxes ranging from empty laundry soap boxes to tampon boxes, would have a widget or pipe cleaner punched through the sides to attach to the stainless steel door. One good rambunctious nose or extended tongue job and the whole container would be strewn over the kennel floor, forcing a frenzied worker to redistribute the contents to the proper overnight guest. The "pussy cat," Orphy, the owl-eyed brawler, Virginia, and the sneaky biter, Jake!

Gerri had a way with animals, and she tolerated their antics, often shrieking, "Aren't they cute!" Cute? Those were not my thoughts when Jake would lift his leg on Gerri's kitchen table. Virginia would wet in Gerri's bed, and Orphy would eat anything that wasn't nailed down and upchuck all over the house. They would be presented for illnesses that were either phantom bugs or just plain baffling events at the Perrault Bed and Breakfast. "I think it was this one, or yet maybe it was the cat that peed on the newspaper!?" I didn't have a clue where to start each investigation.

The garage door was always left open at the Perrault B and B. The double wide would be carefully lifted up at the bottom only about six inches so that all of the neighborhood stray cats could come to eat and have a fresh dinner at any time day or night. The six-inch mark was to limit big dogs or any other large creature access to the smorgasbord. Yeah, right! The only problem with this was that there was no stopping all the local wildlife varmints from helping themselves, too. The words, "Free food at Gerri's," must have spread like wildfire because every raccoon, feral cat, mouse, and chipmunk would gorge its little tummy. Gerri was buying fifty pounds of pet food weekly just for the ones that were coming into her garage at night. She turned on the light one night to find two opossums chowing down at the carefully arranged bowls. The reflective beady shiny eyes of these prehistoric looking little mammas was accompanied by their throaty hissing noise which always makes them sound intimidating. Gerri was rather exasperated when she called the clinic the next morning.

"I can't believe that there would be opossums getting into my garage and eating the cat food. I tried to send the dogs out there, but the hissing scared them, and they ran back into the house." She seemed stunned by their lack of bravery. "Do you think the opossums will be back? I know the dogs at least scared them, but I don't know if enough." She continued, "Those poor cats. No wonder they look like they're not getting enough to eat! What do you think I can do? How am I going to keep the opossums out? Will they be carrying some diseases?"

Oh, she would ask a myriad of questions and not allow me time to answer them. I was always amazed that when I did answer one of the questions, she would quote me for weeks. With an inquiring mind and a faint twitch on her lower left eyelid, she would query, smile, and wait for my professional reaction to her earnest questions. The only problem was that she was dead serious. How did she find me, and how could I be so lucky to have her add some spice to my day?

"Well, how about calling the Humane Society to set a trap in your garage for tonight? They could catch the opossums, and the problem could go away." I thought this was a very logical approach, right? No more opossums or maybe even a raccoon or two less in the neighborhood would help the poor little stray cats get back to a normal life.

Silly me, as the phone rang in the early evening. It was Gerri, and she was concerned. "I did as you said. I had the Humane Society set a trap this afternoon, and they not only caught one but two opossums at the same time!" she rambled.

"Hey, that's great. A two-fer," I smartly said. "So how can I help you tonight?"

"I don't know what to do now; the Humane Society wants to take them away." She tried to think through her predicament.

It seemed quite logical to me. Isn't that why we would have them come out, set a trap, catch the little critters, and then haul them off? "So," I paused to think through what was coming from the other end of the phone line. "Isn't that what we had in mind that they would do?" I carefully treaded water.

"Yes, but when I asked them what they were going to do with them, they said they were going to take them over to George Wyth Park along the river and release them!" She earnestly pleaded for my understanding.

"I think that would be a great resolve for the problem that you are having with them, don't you?" I said, thinking my reinforcement would help the poor Humane Society animal rescue guy.

"But don't you think that would upset the ecological balance in the Park?" She must have thought with her left eye twitching, wondering how I, too, had not thought of the sensitive ecological balance.

I pressed my head and calmly reinforced to her that two more little opossums that were surely a male and a female would do just fine in this large 320-acre park. All God's creatures have a place in this world; these two would just have a new place to inhabit. And by the way, thank goodness for such caring professors who help mold the inquiring minds of our students and still have such compassion for the little four-legged friends along the way.

***

Through the next years, graying of the hair around the muzzle and the hazy cast to the eyes were the only signs that Orphy had lived a long life, but admitting that he was nearing his end was never on Gerri's radar. The old "crotch sniffer" was not as agile and with this latest onset of nuclear sclerosis of the ocular lenses, he had to cock his head even more to see around the crystal floaters in his vitreous chambers.

He had begun to drag his feet, and his claws clicked as they moved through the forward placement of his front feet on the hardwood floors. His nails were long, but the quicks had grown out so far to the ends that trimming them back would have been a bloody, painful experience. His hearing was gone as was the case with many canine seniors, but his olfactory sense was as keen as ever. If a refrigerator door was cracked open three rooms away, he could spring to action from a dead sleep and bolt to the odor wafting from the fridge.

Dr. Perrault was contemplating taking him on a journey to the very northern tip of the upper peninsula of Michigan to attend a niece's wedding. Orphy's failing was obvious. However, his appetite and vital signs on his physical gave me hope that the old fellow would be up to one more car trip to his early puppy stomping grounds. The options were to either leave him with me in the boarding kennel with his housemates, Virginia and Jake, or not make the trip at all. Gerri's emotions and thoughts were spinning and gyrating like a top. She pleaded for my help in making this decision. After several long, agonizing exam room sessions, I came to the conclusion that my opinion would be the final choice.

"Let's give him one more trip, just the two of you back to the Kennesaw peninsula and wading on the shores of Lake Superior," I said with confidence. It was my hope that even though he was failing, he would be able to make the trip by resting in the front seat as a first class passenger. He sat so regally and alert with his seat belt attached to his harness as they backed out of the drive way. He must have known he had the okay for a road trip. Gerri and her navigator were making one more six hundred-mile jaunt together. Their conversation must have been one to cherish.

That afternoon, Virginia and Jake were dropped off for boarding. I peered out the front door to see Orphy sitting in the front passenger seat, seemingly happy to be rid of his annoying canine buds. It was as if the navigator was anxious to take off. With his gray muzzle, hazy eyes, tilted head, and one erect ear and one flopped, the soul mates were ready to hit the road.

With the hubbub of the summer's activity in the clinic, I had put Orphy's travels to the back of my mind. As the afternoon appointments started to come through the front door, the phone rang. Through the motioning of Cali's head and her body language, I sensed that this was a call I should take before I stepped into the room full of spring kittens. Holding her hand over the receiver, she mouthed to me, "It's Gerri, and she's having problems with Orphy!"

"Why me?" I thought as I hurried to the back laboratory desk to take the phone. "Uh, huh," I muttered to a cascade of rapid fire questions. Orphy had made the marathon trip in relatively good condition. He had been helped down out of the van every two hours for leg stretching and to do his business. He had sniffed around the rest stops like a sleuth checking out his territory. Although it was summer, he had not been drinking his water at these frequent rest stops along the way. "Was it due to the air conditioning? Was it the change in the water? Should I have brought along some water from home? Is it because my sister won't let him come in the house and he is having to stay in the garage? Are his kidneys okay?" These were among the queries and thoughts echoing through the ear piece.

"Well, Gerri, I believe you need to take him into the local veterinary practice to get their evaluation," I concluded after considering his history and her concerns. "Tell them your situation. I am sure they will help you and Orphy. They can call me should they need any more background." To some, this directive would have been conclusive, but for Gerri in her state of angst, it was just one more thing to add to the wedding day alternatives.

"But my sister…he's just lying there shivering…poor baby. Do you think he is suffering? Do you think he'll be okay? They think I'm ruining the wedding weekend…poor baby. Do you think I should just come home?" The receiver almost vibrated with her short staccato worries.

"Gerri, I want you to take him into the veterinarian there, and they will help you. I have my directory open, and here is the phone number. They are a multi-veterinarian group practice, and they also see farm animals, so I'm sure they will give you good care and advice," I firmly stated. As I hung the phone up, I cringed to think that this poor veterinarian would have to thumb through all of the drama to help Orphy and Gerri. I could only imagine them trying to sort through the rapid fire questions and what ifs. The old "crotch sniffer" sounded like he was on his last days, and I was not there to help him. I felt guilty that I had given her the go ahead to make the journey. On the other hand, I could be having him die here with me in the boarding kennel. That they were together at least was my ultimate rationalization.

The afternoon appointments took my mind away from my friend in Michigan. I had just seen my last patient who was piddling outside its litter box when, sure enough, I was shaken back to reality. Janie poked her head into the room as I was saying goodbye to Mrs. Walmsley and Michael, her cat. "You have a long distance call from Michigan!"

"Uh huh, I see…yes…well…but you didn't leave him with them?…fluids…kidney failure…make it through the night…didn't want to leave him alone," were all the short snippets of comments I could wedge in among the seemingly endless vibrations being thrown my way. "Well, Gerri, I believe this is critical. Maybe you should have left him at the vet's for the night, but with the intravenous fluids they gave him, he should feel better and will rest better for you tonight. How hot is it in your sister's garage? Is he urinating at all? Is he able to walk? How does he look in the eyes? You say that he's not vomiting and has had a bowel movement?" I could play this question game too. I tried to envision the scene as I spun around on the lab swivel chair, I knew it would not be the last call from Gerri this night.

Sure enough, the first one came at 8:00 PM, another at midnight, and finally at 3:00 in the morning with the ringing at my bedside. "Gerri, you are just going to have to call the vets there. I know since they also do farm animals that they will come to the house there and see Orphy. You just have to act desperate, and they will come and help you," I assured her. My great colleagues are all of the same cut of cloth. We are not only the animal's doctor but equally the human's doctor too. I knew with a little cajoling and pleading, I too would get out of my warm bed in the middle of the night to see a sparrow that had fallen from a tree if the voice on the phone was in distress.

Either I had dozed off and not heard the phone, or yes, the vets had made a middle-of-the-night rescue of Orphy, but the phone had been silent for a few hours. Had I been dreaming, or had these conversations really happened at all? I piled out of bed, shaved, grabbed a cup of coffee and ran out the door. I had just sat down at the desk to catch up on the morning paperwork when the phone message came back to me. "It's Gerri for you." *Lord have mercy on me*, I thought. I took a deep breath and exhaled slowly. I smiled and I answered cheerfully.

"Oh, no Gerri. I'm so sorry. Gosh he went fast...but they did come...I know...but they did the best for him. That was a shock to them I'm sure...Well, they surely have a freezer...You call me and I'll meet you there...right after the wedding...drive all night...Are you sure? I'll be there at seven o'clock...alright. Gerri I'm so sorry. See you in the morning. To say to 'drive safely' sounds trite, but be careful of the deer...goodbye," and I hung the phone back on the hook. I sat for a moment trying to think back on Orphy's final trip home. I probably should have advised her not to take him. At least they had a good first leg of the trip together. This last twenty-four hours of agony and his quick demise were terribly upsetting. I knew how much she worried, and I needed to have been there to support her, but man, she wasn't mad at me but the poor veterinarian that she had awakened in the middle of the night. He picked up Orphy and took him back to the hospital, treated him, and bedded him down during the early morning hours. Gerri was furious though that the vet wouldn't let her stay with Orphy, and he had died there all alone.

I wheeled into the lot as the hazy morning as the fog blanketed the scene. An eerie feeling crossed me as I stepped out of the truck. There was the Perrault van waiting for me at the arranged early Sunday morning hour. Gerri had driven the six hundred miles all night after the Saturday nuptials. She had picked up Orphy's body on the way out of town. She had not changed from her wedding attire and looked frazzled with her mascara now smudged and running down her cheeks. I reached into the window and firmly touched her shoulder with an affectionate silent touch. There was her old friend in a black cadaver bag with his head laying on a pillow and one foot resting on the console.

"His foot may be slightly thawed," she softly confessed. "I held it all of the way."

My eyes welled up as I opened the door to carry him into the clinic. In times like these, it is often best not to say anything. I laid him on the table, made a paw print in a clay mold, and clipped a tuft of his hair to put in a sachet card as a memorial.

Walking Gerri back to her car, I knew the other two dogs would need to stay with me for a few days until she was able to get some sleep and make plans for life at home without the old "crotch sniffer." I waved goodbye and thanked her for sharing her friend with me. He was the best!

The Hat Lady

Nodding back and forth just to see the preacher man on Easter Sunday was common due to the obstructed view caused by the bonnet brigade. In the 1950s, all women with a sense of fashion donned hats for formal settings. Sunday church, weddings, school events, and shower parties of all sorts were hat wearing events. The wardrobe could not be complete without some type of head gear. There were tall ones, disc-shaped, wide brim, feather features, and tight wrap-arounds. Minnie Pearl from the Grand Old Opry fame with her dangling price tag would have gone unnoticed in this early 6:00 AM service.

For this special early sunrise service, I had already been out to the barn to milk the three cows who were surprised to be awakened at such an early hour. The huge Brown Swiss, Red Bomber, and Black Baldy, the black and white Holstein cross, eagerly came into their stanchions as the five coffee can–scoops of grain awaited them. One of my chores was to milk them by hand before and after school. Hearing the pinging, methodical sound hit the bottom of the stainless pails in the quiet morning air was not unlike listening to the first kernels of popcorn hitting the lid on the stove. Back and forth with each hand alternating the squeezing motion, the first half inch of milk in the pail soon developed a foam topping due to the rapid fire streams of milk penetrating the surface. In some ten minutes Swissy could give five gallons of pearly white milk. Combined with the other two cows' milk, it would be run through the DeVale cream separator. My hands and arms would become extremely strong which came in handy as I could take on all comers in arm wrestling.

After the processional and the trumpets playing taps that echoed in the distance, I would lay my head on my dad's shoulder, feigning to look around the hats, and would doze off. I always wondered why he would allow this until I glanced up to see his head nodding and eyes closed too.

The ladies' hat fashion had waned in its popularity and style by the 1970s. Mrs. Kay Ray had made an appointment for Bonnie, her senior brown Heinz 57 mixed breed spaniel. She aimed her mammoth two-toned Cadillac around the street corner and came to halt in the parking lot. Out of the car, adorned in a pink dress and a wide brimmed pink hat, stepped a genteel, attractive lady in her seventies. Her jewelry sparkled and accented every open area of flesh. Her makeup was under coated with layers of emollients and powders. She had no aging wrinkles, and a pink pastel lipstick accented her beautiful face.

A debutante daughter of a prominent manufacturing company, Mrs. Ray had been one of the last models and style review performers at the large Black's Department store. Black's was not the size or fame of Macy's, but it was the local store where well-to-do women shopped for the latest and greatest dresses hitting the fashion world. Mrs. Ray never went anywhere without being dressed to the nines—a trademark hat always topped her blonde–tinted French–rolled hair.

I had seen her at the local Methodist church, always sitting in the second row back from the organ. Our family sat in the balcony, peering down from above. The obvious standout was the "hat lady," as our girls would call her.

She was a widow, having married late in life to a man in the construction business. He provided for them well, and her family's fortune allowed her to live on the Cedar River along a wooded vista. She had found our office following a fall in which she had broken her hip. Bonnie had boarded with us during Kay's convalescene. Two or three times every day, Kay would call and want to talk to Bonnie. Cali and I would faithfully go the suite and bring Bonnie to the phone. Holding the receiver to her ear, Bonnie would shake her head and excitedly wiggle at Kay's voice echoing from the other end. Bonnie would whine with excitement as Kay told her how much she loved her and missed her and that she would be back soon.

During these times, it was not uncommon to be hospitalized with a broken hip for several weeks. Bonnie became used to her new setting and would send pink flowers to Kay a few times to brighten up her recovery room at Sartori Hospital.

First the walker, then the cane, and finally back to driving, Kay made a full recovery. Bonnie, however, was running out of time. First her hearing waned, then her eyesight faded, and then one day she died suddenly in her sleep in her pink-lined crib. I rushed out to the Cottage Row home to find Mrs. Ray in a very reflective state. Though she was still in her morning pink negligee, her makeup was immaculate, with a sparkly barrette fashionably placed in her chignon hairdo. She was not nearly as weepy as I had forethought. She pointed out to the row of wooden handmade crosses on the elevated terrace in the garden. Bonnie would be the thirteenth one in that cemetery. Tom, her caretaker gardener, had already dug the grave, and all seemed to be in order. I was astonished that she had this many dogs from the past. There were no more living with her, but that wouldn't last for long.

***

"Her name is Sparky," Kay giggled as she held her close to her bosom. "I found her through a friend of a friend. She's seven years old, and isn't she gorgeous!"

"Wow, Mrs. Ray, if a little dog could wear a hat, she would be the one," I observed. Sparky was a white mix with surely some poodle blood and some maltese added, giving her white flowing hair. She held her head so alert and confidently. She knew she was not just cute but special. A Princess! A Lady! She was every bit as elegant and stylish as Mrs. Ray. She had pink lipstick adorning her muzzle and forehead from Kay smooching and caressing her.

For the next ten years, Sparky Ray would be in to see us on an almost weekly routine. Her biweekly grooming appointments with Becky were classic events. Kay with her beautiful hats, Sparky with her rhinestone collar, lipstick marks, and the big Cadillac all made for a classic scene.

Sparky was a hypochondriac. However, the poor little princess is not to be blamed. If Sparky would blink wrong, the procession to the vet was immediate. Her upset stomach, watering eyes, slightly soft BMs, turning her nose up at her food, growling GI noises, scratching at her sides, smelly ears, halitosis, licking her toes were among the normal complaints.

Mrs. Ray and Sparky could have been the leading act in any parade through town. The queen with her mammoth pink hat and the netting shading her eyes, and the Princess with her jeweled collar batting her eyes for the spectators. I had never seen a person so dedicated and in love with such a pretty little dog in my lifetime. Sparky and Kay, Kay and Sparky, they were synonymous. I cringed and knew that the day was coming when "all the king's horses and all the king's men" couldn't put Sparky back together again. As she slowed and her body began to fail, she still had a beautiful face and physique. Her groomings washed away her oily hair. After a combing out, she had lustrous white hair. She continued to defy her age. She seemed to smile and gently closed her eyes in appreciation and understood she was the most beautiful dog on the planet.

The final day came, and Sparky, like her predecessor passed away quietly in her sleep. My building manager and animal attendant, Gene, made a pine wood coffin for her. He engraved her name on the cover and helped Mrs. Ray decide where this new grave should be placed.

Two days later, my wife, Cynthia, and I made a home visit to take Mrs. Ray some cinnamon rolls and flowers. She greeted us still in her mourning time. I had never seen her in anything but pink or bright yellows or greens. Donning a black gown, her face was drawn and looked weary. She had a hanky in her hand to dab her eyes and face when an occasional memory of Sparky would cause her to be overcome. I had no idea that she had not buried Sparky by now, until she said, "Would you like to see her?"

I looked at Cynthia, and she nodded, "of course." We followed Mrs. Ray into her bedroom. There was Sparky laying on her side in a white bassinette. Her torso was draped with a satin pink coverlet. A few bubbles had started to come out of her nose and Kay touched them nonchalantly to remove them with her hanky.

"Doesn't she look natural?" she uttered adoringly as we embraced.

The Broadway performance of *Cats* has a song about the Great Mr. Mistoffelees that goes "there never ever will be another like Great Mr. Mistoffelees." If one day Andrew Lloyd Weber writes the musical *Dogs*, Sparky will have a leading role as the Great, Beautiful, Beloved, Miss Sparky Ray.

Poor Old Blue

Mr. VanDuvall was knocking at our back door. He was a large African American farmer, 6'3", dressed in Big Smith blue bib overalls. He loomed like a giant waiting for me to answer his knock. I had jumped up from the dinner table when I heard the dog barking, and a pickup come into the driveway. He asked as I opened the door, "Is your Pa here? I came to deliver the boar."

"Yep, come on in. We're still at the supper table," I said, as I welcomed him in through the porch, through the kitchen, and into the family dining room. I had never met him before. His huge frame filled the rooms as he moved through our old farm house. He had to duck down as the stairs to the top level of the house projected down into the ceiling of the hallway.

"Dad," I called, "a man is here to see you about a pig."

They greeted each other, and he pulled up a chair to have dessert with us. Verna hurried back to the kitchen to get another plate of apple crisp and a cup and saucer for coffee.

I listened intently as my dad and Phil VanDuvall visited about the boar which he had brought to sell to us. They talked about getting some seed corn before he left. My father had a small DeKalb seed dealership that provided the area farmers a ready source to pick up a bag or two of hybrid milo or corn at their convenience. It was a chance for my father to visit with the neighbors during the winter and get preorders. As was often the case, he also worked as a banker, because he sometimes did not get paid for the bag of seed until the grain was harvested some four to five months later.

We unloaded the rangy black and white belted Hampshire boar into the open pen adjacent to the two Hamp gilts that we had bought from my Uncle Ivan. I was giddy with excitement as I anticipated them being mated and the coming of baby pigs. I had cleaned and bedded the pens with fresh bright orange oat straw. Pigs and straw are like kids at the park—They grab a wedge of straw in their mouths and shake it vigorously, spreading the loosened straws through the air. They dance and frolic, doing 360s like they are hallucinating.

Moving to Iowa where pigs and corn were king, I was awed by the big farms and their specialties in livestock production. Some farms were breeding–to–market operations where others only raised the piglets to twenty-five pounds and let finishers take them all the way to market weight at around 250 pounds.

Management, production, feed efficiency, nutrition, an understanding of environmental buildings, and disease control were all facets of knowledge needed by a veterinarian.

When having so many different production models, dealing with the human element became the essential component in all operations. A rather crude diagnosis of PPM could be used to describe some supposed disease conditions. Farmers and veterinary jargon often used initials to shorten disease symptoms such as TGE, MMA, PPE, EEE, VEE, and WEE which were all used with authority, whether or not the farmer had a grasp on their meaning. So when describing PPM, some degree of discretion and tongue in cheek had to accompany its use. Piss Poor Management could describe why there was disease symptoms on any level of livestock production. During good times of high commodity prices, the price of pork, beef, or milk could offset some of the less-than-perfect management, and a farm would still see cash flow. But on the flipside of good prices, PPM was often the magnifier and resulted in cutting corners and trying to cheapen the input costs.

Failing to vaccinate for certain diseases simply because of neglect or cost of the vaccine was a deterrent and a guarantee of problems down the road. Corn picker's disease was another malady that came into some livestock settings in the fall, when all of the effort in combining the corn in the short windows of good weather caused neglect in some of the daily chores of the farm.

Blue, a tough, blocky looking linebacker blue heeler was waiting for me as I opened the exam door. Dick Gerke was his owner, and Blue went with him everywhere. He was a cattle dog and helped Dick with the hog chores too. His encouraging nip at the heels of the Angus cows and his intimidating bark and guarding of the open gates made him as vital as a hired man at times.

Blue was not himself. He was listless, and a long, shiny string of saliva was dangling from the corner of his lip. "Hey, old guy. You don't look so good today," was my first greeting as he stood in the corner by the examination table. His face was placid, and with his eyes squinted, he stared into space. He exhibited a slight tremor and sat stoically on his back haunches.

Dick was a stubborn German farmer who was struggling to make ends meet on his land and livestock operation. He raised Angus cattle and was at the height of his glory when we processed and worked with his purebred calves in the spring and fall. He explained that Blue was okay yesterday, but today when going into the barn, Blue was not the first to greet him. The hog buildings were next to the cattle sheds and formed a close cluster of buildings on the farmstead. Jane, Dick's wife, had been the primary caregiver on the farrowing side of the business during the fall corn harvest season. She had been the one who let the sows in and out of the farrowing crates twice daily to allow exercise and cleaning of the stalls. She had done an immaculate job in cleaning and washing the water cups and bedding down with new aromatic wood shavings. The baby pigs would huddle under the suspended heat lamps and went crazy when the new shavings were dropped into the side pens for them to lay on. Dick reported that Jane had been losing a lot of pigs recently. Some just stopped eating, and others would have a trembling and body shaking motion and would be dead in a few hours. The pile of dead piglets was accumulating outside the farrowing house.

As I looked at Blue and then Dick, I knew immediately that this was not good. Not only was Blue going to die, but Dick had a mess on his hands at home too. "Dick," I slowly opened, "Blue has pseudorabies. He has gotten it from the pigs. He is not infectious to any other animal or human, however. Dogs are considered a dead-end host for pseudorabies, but that is just it. He is going to die of this encephalitic virus. I can't help him."

Dick dropped his head to his chest and pulled out his red soiled handkerchief from is back pocket. Having such a proud man in tears in my presence was not unusual when bad news of impending death of a pet was revealed. I put my arm around him and slowly kept talking to support him in time of remorse.

"I am so sorry; we do have a remedy for the pigs, but we have to act quickly." This news was a small consolation, but losing Blue was tragic. It appeared that Blue had taken one of the dead baby pigs back to his barn and chewed on the dead carcass. This had given him direct contact with the pseudorabies virus.

I asked if Jane would like to see Blue one more time, and Dick shook his head no. He hugged his old friend one more time and blubbered, "I love you. I'm going to miss you, old friend." These were always the times that my eyes watered too. I cradled Blue to take him away for good.

Pseudorabies or "like" rabies would run rampant for another twenty years in the hog populations of Iowa. I would see tens of thousands of hog deaths. Cattle, dogs, and cats were extremely susceptible to its infection too. A federal blood testing program was undertaken by the United States Department of Agriculture and has effectively eliminated the virus.

Dick and Jane helped me inoculate all the pigs on the farm with a modified live virus—an outbreak could be stopped cold in its tracks within a few hours with this vaccination program.

Old Mr. VanDuvall who had sold us a boar in exchange for some seed corn would have been awed at such a miracle vaccine. Oh, the innocence of rural life! And yet, the dramatic extent of a deadly disease spreading like wildfire made the veterinarian and the farmer partners in our love for animals.

Dog Gone

Right up there with never saying, "I have no clue what's wrong with your animal," is the fear or embarrassment of having to admit to a trusting owner that their pet escaped the protective care of the veterinary hospital.

It is just one of those things that happens in every veterinarian's life. It was like saying, "I have never lost a cow when treating for milk fever," to veteran vet, who would then retort "Then you just haven't treated enough of them, yet!"

Such innocence to the novice was first brought to my experience in Lake Geneva, Wisconsin, in 1974. I was doing my summer internship in a large four-veterinarian dairy practice. Heartworm disease in dogs had become the biggest epidemic to come to the veterinary profession since hog cholera, Bangs disease in cattle, and distemper in dogs.

Heartworms were just that, a parasite that was carried by mosquitos and transferred from canine to canine by the blood sucking proboscis of the mosquito. In those summer small animal clinic hours, a blood test taken from the dog's leg would reveal the small swimming microfilaria or baby heartworms under a microscope. It seemed to be at its peak epidemic times as we would diagnose between three to four cases every week. The more we tested, the more positive results we found.

The treatment for heartworms was four intravenous injections of an arsenic solution spaced at twelve hour increments while hospitalized in a quiet kennel. The protocol was stringent, and owners were counseled that their dog must be kept quiet and resting at all times during treatment.

Thunder was an oversized black lab weighing nearly one hundred pounds. He was not overweight but had the body and frame of a middle linebacker. If he had been suited up for football, there wouldn't have been a helmet large enough because this guy had a mammoth, honking big head. The owners had driven up from Illinois. They warned that he was an escape artist and that he didn't like to be confined. These instructions were given to the veterinary receptionist and the attending veterinarian. Assurances were given that we would watch him closely. "He will be just fine, do not worry, and we'll take good care of him."

The next morning as Dr. Both was drawing up the thick syrupy arsenic solution, I opened Thunder's run to slip a leash around his neck and lead him up to the treatment table. I couldn't have been hit harder by an all-American fullback as he saw just a crack in the gate opening to make his escape. He had to have planned this all night, as the dress rehearsal was the real thing. I was stunned as I rocked back, still holding the leash in one hand and the support bar on the door with the other. I peered to my right to see a flashing tail disappear around the corner. I surely must have yelled something like, "Dog loose! Shut the door! Help, get him!" I heard the slipping of claws peeling out on the linoleum flooring. As I recovered my balance and took flight after him, it seemed like the only thing I would ever see was an extended tail blitzing around another corner. Doors slammed. Chip, the technician in the laboratory, came to attention. Dr. Both dropped the arsenic bottle to the counter, and the receptionist screamed.

With the early morning rays beaming in the east facing picture windows in the waiting room, the surreal dust particles and hair floating in the air seemed like distant stars in the planetary system. This would be the last stand. Several clients with lap dogs grasped them to their bosoms. They appeared frozen in time as the drama unfolded in slow motion. With one more lightning lap around the waiting room, Thunder hit the screen door at the wooden crossbar and burst out into the driveway, across two lanes of the highway, and into the high grass pasture adjacent.

The Keystone Kops were onto his scent like some clumsy blood hounds. Dr. Both with his slow drawl and always calm demeanor jumped in his practice vet van. Dr. Houck raced to his big truck with the mobile vet box and yelled that he'd go around the section to head the dog off. Like heading this rocket-powered animal off at the pass was going to stop him. Dr. Grover had me jump in his side door to the veterinary mobile van, and we headed south in a pincher movement.

Just to the southeast of the clinic, about two miles away, was the Lake Geneva Playboy Club. It had two eighteen-hole golf courses, riding stables, tennis courts, and a ski hill, all surrounding the exclusive James Bond–style hotel and resort.

The dragnet posse pursued this now mass of black protoplasm. Sure, keep him quiet while undergoing the heartworm treatment crossed each of our minds, but the chase had to take precedence. An occasional sighting would whet our appetites and give us new hope for a rescue. The adrenalin pumped and each of the posse had new ideas. It was like "all Indians and no chief" or maybe the three Stooges with the summer intern student kid that enveloped the Playboy Club. I mounted a big gelding from the stable and coaxed him up the steep ski hill to get a higher vantage point of the playing field and golf courses below. Houck commandeered a Cessna 186 and was piloted for an aerial reconnaissance. If time had permitted, I'm sure we would have thought of dropping leaflets in the surrounding countryside. Not to be outdone, Dr. Both jumped on a golf cart to dart around the course. Bewildered golfers would see his panic as he buzzed up to them, asking if they'd seen a big black dog.

No luck. No dog. The trail and scent had evaporated. No Thunder. I assumed the poor guy must have exhausted himself and lay down and died as the heartworms released into his lungs.

The four of us converged on the security gate at the same time. The two-way radios had been chattering cold leads and new attack plans for over two hours. Farm calls were waiting for all of us, and finding Thunder had exhausted our cumulative wits. Duty called. The hunt was called off.

During the rest of the day in-between dairy calls, each veterinarian cruised back to the scene to knock on doors of the rural homes. No one reported any sightings. Dog Gone! Thunder gone! The scent had gone cold.

A difficult call was made to the owners to tell them of the accidental runaway, Thunder. They did not seem as upset as we all did. They suggested that he just might return to the clinic later in the day as it was the last place he knew. They reassured us that he was a really smart dog. Smart was not what we had been calling him all day in his absence. They said they would bring up his blanket, some toys, and his favorite food to drop it off at the clinic front door, perchance that he would circle back.

Little hope was given for his return. No phone calls reporting a darting black bullet sprinting through the fields was forthcoming. On the other side, no dead black dog reports had come either.

The clear cool summer evening had set in after such a hectic day. Dr. Grover picked me up from the rental mobile home. We were off to an early evening emergency about a horse that had got caught up in some barbed wire. Being the intern, I was always eager to go on any after hour emergencies. Just for good measure, we headed back toward the clinic to see if Thunder's owners had left the promised blanket and toys on the steps of the office.

As we made the turn and descended into the office gravel lot, there was an Illinois plated station wagon. Just ahead were two children and Mom and Dad. Making licking rounds between them as they sat there in a circle was Thunder. Gosh, what a day! And forty years later, the welts I incurred from the sweat bees on top of the horse on the ski hill seem to get larger every time I think of this goofy dog and his heartworm disease.

Thunder would not be the last dog to escape my care. He was the only one however, that would spend the whole day at a Playboy Club. In later years, I would chase after a Bully, Truffles, Pongo, and Pierre, but nothing would compare to Thunder.

Billy the Dreamer

Billy Joe wore his red cap at every position on his head. In the winter, it would be a heavy red and black checkered one with the ear flaps that could be tied up over the top. The rest of the year, it would be just a seed company ball cap that showed the dust and sweat of outdoor hard work. Sometimes the bill of the monogramed front would be at ninety degrees. Other times he would have the cap on backwards. Then the next time I would see him, it would be pointing at three o'clock. He was a young farmer, yet had a large cattle and hog operation. Together with his wife, Esther May, they lived out in the country seven miles from town. My father had two cattle pastures nearby, and often one of our cows would go missing. Certain cows could find a weak spot in the barbed wire fence or a creek washout to escape the perimeter of our pasture. Father and I would stop to check with the Wooster's to see if they had seen the "old rip" or the "breechy old cow" as my father would call the missing one.

Billy Joe and Esther were just getting started in their farming ventures in the 1950s and lived in a quaint ten- by twenty-foot wooden structure. We affectionately called it the chicken house. Whether or not it had ever been, it was painted neatly in a bright barn red and trimmed immaculately with white around the door and two east-facing windows. Each dollar made on this farm went back into more cattle, more machinery, and buying more adjacent land. Out back was the beginning of a boarded up foundation which was to become their new house. Billy had this thing about starting a project and having about 10 other distractions before ever getting back to the original job. It seemed to take him about three years to complete the house, but as was common of the times, it was paid for the day they moved from the "chicken house" to the big house. Had it not been for multiple babies coming along, I'm sure they would still be working on finishing the house.

A dreamer, a worker, and a consummate optimist, Billy Joe was nonstop. Be it poor prices, drought, flooding streams, gulley washers, crop failures, or diseases, Billy Joe would have given Job a run for his money. Billy Joe's rosy outlook carried him through even the most difficult times.

Another Bill would cross my path and give me a ride through his dreams and animal ventures. Bill, Sr. as his son was a Billy too, was not unlike my childhood Billy Joe, the Kansas farmer.

Before there is any negative connotation about his occupation, I will just say that Bill Colwell was a used car salesman, and if that would ever be used disparagingly on a person's background, he did not fit the picture.

Bill was loud. He had a booming, room-filling voice and through his wire rims, his eyes danced with enthusiasm and vitality. His ever present tan canvas fedora, plaid work shirt, khaki jeans, and cowboy work boots made his presence bigger than life. He seemed to always be in a hurry, and I could not imagine him ever stopping to sleep or much less eat. His rounded barrel chest and tummy were evidence that he did not lack for nourishment.

Bill's many years of car sales had given him a nice disposable income. His computer-like mind gave him a genius mathematic ability to compute a profit line into any deal, whether that be in the automobiles, real estate, or livestock. He had been broke and rich more than once in this past, but neither had ever tainted his ability to be positive about tomorrow.

When I met him, he was in his mid-50s. He proudly professed that he had given up his beer habit and two-pack-a-day smoking addiction. I am sure he did both cold turkey as his determination was monumental.

I was called to his rural acreage to vaccinate and tubeworm his quarter horses. I had no idea that driving over the cattle guard gate and down the lane lined with neat sucker rod metal fencing would lead me into the dreamer's stables. These quarter horses weren't run of the mill horses. They had pedigrees and credentials that would make royalty proud. The two stallions were high-energy, rambunctious, power driven steeds. They paced in their individual stalls and snorted their disapproval at this unknown vet coming into their stable.

"Geez, they must know you're a vet," Bill observingly announced.

"Yeah, I don't know what it is, but they always seem to know," I said. I only half believed this because I believe any stranger would have set them off in the same manner.

Bill was proud of his horses but told me that the quarter horse market had "gone to pot," and it wasn't worth his time to breed them anymore because he wasn't able to get rid of the foals. Having a stallion and brood mares is a dangerous combination. Stallions go crazy with fire and lust when there is a mare in heat or the presence of estrogen in the air. I couldn't imagine Bill having the time, patience, and ability to have them together to mate and breed in a small barn and arena. I even got the feeling that he was insecure or afraid of them as we commenced to catch each one to treat them with a physical exam, vaccinations, and wormer.

Auscultating the chest of the smoke-blowing, nervous palomino stud was a challenge. In between Bill's "Stop it damnit—I said stop it!" and my concerns that Bill not get his feet wrapped up in the long dangling lead rope as Rocket danced on the end of his halter, I carefully placed the bell of the stethoscope on his side. The throbbing pulse of the heart valves was loud and distinct. "How the heck did I ever get myself into this?" was my next thought. Tube worming a horse was considered the gold standard for getting the worming medication into the stomach. Since other medications are often given to a horse via this method, it was a convenient skill for a veterinarian to possess. Placing a well-lubricated three quarter inch tube into the ventral turbinate of the left nostril of a horse requires some skill and cajoling even to a docile, plug-headed horse. To consider doing this to a wild-eyed, steam-blowing, testosterone overloaded bronc is another thing altogether. With a metal twitch attached to his muzzle, I told Bill to hold on tight and if the horse resisted, to squeeze a little harder. I bravely wetted the stomach tube in a stainless steel bucket of cold water and ratcheted my hand down to the tapered end.

Both bravery and stupidity should be used to describe such operations because it really takes both to complete this maneuver. There once was a deodorant commercial that said, "Don't ever let 'em see you sweat." This was one of those moments. Holding the warm pink snorting nostril open with the right hand, the tube was passed beneath the index finger into the small ventral opening of the turbinate. Using short and quick propelling movements it passed to the back of the nose over the palate into the back of the mouth cavity. Whew, half way home. Rocket's eyes enlarged with indignation as if to say, "What in the heck are you doing to me now?" The next part of this procedure was to get the tough guy to swallow the end of the tube so that it went into the esophagus and not the windpipe trachea opening. "Okay, big guy," I mumbled while blowing on the other end, "this is where I need your help." By rotating the tube ninety degrees clockwise and giving a short tap of the tip on the back of the phalanx, he swallowed the tube, hook, line, and sinker. As I watched from the side of the neck, the tube progressed down inside of the esophagus like a mole crossing new grass. As it entered into the stomach, I took my tongue out of the other end of the tube as it released the rush of air from the gastric passage. Beautiful! The smell of slightly fermented green grass was the cardinal sign that the tube had hit pay dirt and was not down the forbidden trachea and into the lungs. The funnel was put in place as the wormer was poured down into the descending Two rinses with water and a final blow on the tube to push the residual contents into the stomach, and the ordeal was over. By holding a thumb over the distal opening, I pulled the tube back up the passage, through the phalanx, and stripped out of the nose opening. All three of us could breathe again; Rocket, an amazed Bill, and myself.

Bill was impressed and admitted he really didn't think I would ever get this done on his prized stud. He didn't know that my knees were a little unsteady, but I always believed that an animal would always take advantage of you if you ever let them know you were afraid of them. So much for the phrase "Discretion is the better part of valor!" We proceeded to tube the other seven horses, and Bill thought I had passed the test.

We had many more exciting adventures at "Wild Bill's Ranch". Somehow the Angus cattle that grazed these rolling glaciated slopes lost their original challenge. They required daily feeding, housing, bedding, and occasionally a rodeo to separate and move them between pastures. They were of the best Black Angus registered stock, but the animal husbandry and reward of ownership were inversely proportional.

Bill had me castrate a thousand-pound bull calf behind a steel paneled gate while squeezing him between a wall and the gate. Holding a cow or calf's tail directly up over the back has a way of anesthetizing the nerve sensation to the perineal region and all the way down the back end to the scrotum. By positioning directly behind this beast, a standing castration can be done without getting killed. These are famous last words as both of those hind legs loom, loaded and ready to blast backwards to nail anything within reach. "Push hard and keep that tail forward at 180 degrees," I admonished him. Bill was dripping sweat, and this was wintertime. The sharp scalpel, which I held between my teeth, was removed to make short deliberate swipes across the bottom of the sac. Both huge jewels were removed without any excess bleeding. I slid out of the way to safety, and the gate was released for this yearling—now steer—to run back to the paddock wondering what had just happened.

The Angus herd was sold. Santa Gertrudis cattle were purchased from the King Ranch in Texas. These gorgeous reddish brown cows are a breed that was developed at the King Ranch. They are a cross between a Brahma and Red Angus, and feature the Brahma characteristics of huge drooping ears, a long face, dolloping brisket skin, and a slight hump on their withers. They are spooky, too. Much like Superman, they can clear a ten-foot fence with a single leap. Other than that, they are beautiful creatures to lay one's eyes upon. One significant problem with the breed is that they are very thin skinned. Thin skin and below fifty-degree weather don't go well together, not to mention freezing, zero, and the minus below that was prevalent in Iowa during the winter. What a challenge for this young veterinarian they would be! Running them through an alley into a cattle chute was really exciting work, especially when the help that was promised from the old car salesman's office would not show up, or when they were petrified by the sight of a thousand-pound steam-rolling, four-legged body barreling its way toward the gate opening. The "Drama the Brahma" ordeal only made it one winter as they shivered and snorted their way to spring before being transported back south to a warmer climate. With the deal, several used cars were undoubtedly exchanged.

The Santa Gertrudis were replaced by twenty longhorn calves. I had no proof and didn't ask Bill, but I concluded again that there was some more trading of four wheels that went along with this deal. The old car shark had probably gotten a few nice trade-ins, as he seldom failed to come out smelling like a rose.

The longhorns were much easier to work with than the red colored cousins from the King Ranch, though they also had issues with the temperatures at this latitude for the winter months. None of the cattle developed the classic rack of horns as seen across the doors in museums or mantels in rustic ranch scenes. Overnight, these yearling longhorns were dispersed. More trade-ins were to be assumed. I never asked details but knew the novelty and enjoyment of raising and nurturing these Chisolm trail creatures would soon be replaced with another dream.

Soon there came llamas, wild sika deer, miniature donkeys, and black swans with their own concrete aerated lined pond. I always wondered if maybe lions, tigers, and bears would follow.

I received a weekend call from an excited Bill. "What do you know about elk?"

I knew it was a rhetorical question, but I was caught blindsided so returned, "About as much as you know. Why?" With Bill, there was never any deliberation or negotiation. He had his dream, and I knew from the sound of his voice the elk were on their way.

"Can you come out today, and I'll show you what I am thinking?" he giddily replied.

He had purchased a sandy parcel of land a few miles north of the Wild Bill Ranch and remodeled the accompanying house for his dear and loving wife, Marcia. She was very refined and rarely involved herself in the dreamer's escapades and business dealings. Bill loved her immensely and was a teddy bear in her presence. It was quite the scene to see this Rambo rough and tough cowboy turn into a soft-spoken gentleman when around her. "Yes, Dear. No, Dear. Whatever you want, Dear." Only God could have brought these two together.

Pulling under the wooden archway gate to the Colwell Elk Ranch was like entering Knott's Berry Farm. A long, winding concrete driveway was lined with shrubs and ornamentals perfectly planted and mulched. Interspersed silver maples were neatly supported by guide wires to allow for their support—the dreams of a tree lined promenade for the future years. In the paddock there was a newly constructed Butler building with sun penetrating panels. New, stylish fencing leading to it from all sides corralled the passive donkeys and llamas grazing in the plush orchard grass meadow.

Bill proudly emerged from his shop and office when he heard the truck approaching. His smile went from ear to ear. I could tell he was about ready to bust a button to share his latest.

"Hey, this new driveway, corrals, and all. Man, you must have made a killing on those Longhorns! What did you have to pull to get this one past Marcia?" I needled him as I leaned out of the pickup window.

"Doc, honest this is what she wanted. I had nothing to do with it," he laughed and winked.

"Good grief, Bill, this is an unbelievably beautiful setting. I hope the tax man can't find this place," I grinned and stood in awe looking out over the landscape.

"Just wait till you see the barn. And, oh by the way, there are twenty-five elk cows arriving tomorrow from Pennsylvania," he rather timidly included as we sped off to check out the new barn.

I knew better than to act surprised at any of the dreamer's antics. There around the 80 acres were paddocks with eight-foot high woven wire and majestically placed ten-foot high womanized posts. Even those wild Santa Gertrudis would have been intimidated by these barriers. At the time, Bill related that these structures had cost $20,000 per mile. I never calculated how many miles that would have been, as the property now was separated into four perfectly designed pastures with mammoth gates to funnel the arriving elk from one pasture to the next.

The barn had a herringbone octagonal working pen set up for processing these wild beasts. The panels were solid plywood attached to one-inch rectangular gates so that there was no visual contact for the elk to the outside. Each gate was constructed so that when opened, it could push the half ton creatures from pen to pen with relative ease. The catwalk over the top of the pens allowed a worker with a long wooden pole with a red cloth attached to carefully maneuver and separate these nervous elk. There was a specially designed hydraulic chute, which allowed for treatment, blood testing, and horn or rack removal. To get and keep the elk in the chute with its head caught between the pinching head gate, the side panels squeezed in and the whole animal elevated. This left the fierce sounding wapiti with its feet suspended, head caught, snugged in from the sides and top. Only its cooing vocalization would be heard once restrained.

An elk's thick, sheened hair is at least one-inch long. It can shed water much like a duck's back. It is soft as a feather and has a musky sweet smell of the wild. Its eyes are huge and show fear as they rotate rapidly to get a sense of the surroundings. Elk have such poor peripheral eyesight that they must constantly move their upright heads to survey the situation from all sides.

"Why me?" I thought as I walked through this one of a kind facility. "How could I have been so lucky to be exposed to this kind of animal?" The dreamer had built a fantasyland unlike any other in the central United States.

The herd would eventually expand to 125 cows and bulls. Whenever I thought that it couldn't get any bigger, Bill would fly off to Montana or Canada to buy more of these trumpeting prizes. He was able to manage them all by himself. All the gold in Fort Knox could not have brought any more pleasure than to see him on a crisp, frosty morning, walking among the cows in the pasture. Their bugling could be heard from miles away.

"Okay, you need the whole herd blood tested," as I nodded while listening on the telephone. "Bill, let me check with the State and Feds to make sure we cover all of the restrictions before we do this. Yes...Brucellosis, Tuberculosis, wasting disease, anaplasmosis; Identification...metal ear clip...tattoo...wormer...vitamins...anything else you can think of? Good enough. I'll be there Monday. Early...sounds good." Hurried conversations like this occurred often when Bill needed to get the herd certified so he could sell his calves and seed stock across state lines. This was where his eventual payback for this tremendous investment would come to fruition.

The before dawn roundup and herding into the elk barn was all done by only Bill. He alone could slowly and methodically walk in a circle around the elegant-featured critters to encourage them toward the opened gate. The chilly morning stillness was penetrated by the steam emitted from the nostrils of some one hundred elk staring at their master. Bill carefully talked and reassured them that everything was going to be all right. It only took one cow to spot the opening and see it as an escape route. She took a few guarded steps and the then began to lope with her head held high. Running so elegantly, this lead cow was instantaneously followed by one or two more. Always with their heads swiveling and their eyes noting every movement around them, the rest of the herd spied the leaders making their way toward the gate. They responded and turned tail to stampede for the exit as if they didn't want to be left behind.

The narrowing alleyway system was lined with eight-foot high plywood so that the elk did not catch sight of any distractions or human movement on the outside. The gates and runways were designed to flow the nervous animals toward and into the barn, octagonal pens, and processing chute. Each perfectly positioned gate, handle, and pivoting hinge allowed Bill to do this entire roundup by himself without raising his voice or flapping his arms. The thundering of hooves, clouds of dust, and the clicking of their teeth were the only evidence that such a capture had taken place.

Bill then maneuvered eight to ten cows into each of the octagonal holding pens and anxiously paced until I pulled up in Little Red. My headlights bounced through the faint ground fog as the early sunlight peaked its way through the trees. The morning frost on the prairie grass was like an Andrew Wyeth painting—the stillness of the scene made me want to breathe in its beauty.

"They're all ready for you, Doc," Bill calmly declared. His demeanor did not reflect any of the previous hours of roundup and sorting. What a system, what a man, what a dreamer! His voice was not as loud as usual, and his normally confident spirit seemed subdued.

A helper from the car shop arrived and we commenced to move one cow at a time into the hydraulic chute, catch her in the head gate, and elevate her off the ground. Reading the ear tattoo by placing a flashlight on the backside of the ear to illuminate through the skin and cartilage was done to identify each one. The dangling all-flex numbered tag in the other ear was cross-matched to confirm each one's individual identity. Blood was drawn from the facial vein, which was located across the bridge of the nose. The blood was placed in tubes to be taken back to the clinic for processing and the paper work prepared. All of it would be overnighted to the state lab in Des Moines. Titers would be done to assure there was not Brucellosis, anaplasmosis, or CWD in any of the animals on the farm. Finally, we administered a vitamin injection and a pour-on de-lice and wormer to the back midline of each cow.

This was to be the last time that a complete herd test was to be performed. This certification procedure was the mandated federal regulation required to become a disease-free herd.

We worked from 7:00 AM until dark, only stopping for a short sandwich lunch. The morning labor and hard work had allowed us to get fifty-two elk through in five hours. At that pace, we knew another seven hours would be needed to finish the job. Bill was in his 60s, and his energy and stamina was never in question. He seemed quieter on this day, but his love for these animals was unending. All he had done in his life seemed to be wrapped up in this operation. I was some twenty years younger than Bill at this time, yet as I dragged myself into the final blood drawing, I could only marvel at this man's endurance. He walked me to the truck and thanked me again for the day's work. All told, 120 cows and five bulls had gone through the chute. They were all perfectly healthy, and no injuries had occurred. This was testament to the quality of the working design and Bill's meticulous husbandry care.

"Doc, I have to tell you something before you leave," he slowly droned as the sweat still glistened over his brow. "Some doctor at Mayo says I have lung cancer—but they think they can get it." *Ah ha!* I thought I had noticed just a small change in this proud guy's attitude.

"Dang it, Bill. I am so sorry. When do you go back for the next consultation? How can I help out here? Does Marcia know the extent of this?" My questions churned inside of me.

"Yeah, Bill Junior is aware, and we'll go back next week for a plan. I'm sure I can beat this, but it sure does put a crimp in things. Doc, I've led a hard old life in the past, but I never thought the Big C would ever catch me."

Those words would stick in my ears as the headlights pointed me down the long driveway. A melancholy cloud hung over me as I got back to the clinic and sorted the blood and paperwork for shipment.

I visited Bill at his home some two months later. He was propped up in his bed with pillows on every side. His wire rims were held in place by his beaked nose. I had never seen him without his hat. Gone, too, was the color in his cheeks and his booming voice. His eyes showed the seriousness of his condition. "Well, Doc, I think I've made my last roundup," he proudly and confidently announced. Through teary eyes, I squeezed his feet to tell him, "Man, you have been a wonderful part of my life, and God has blessed us both."

As I saw him there in his casket, I reflected on his immense love for all of the creatures that he had cared for. His profile, with that nose, the wire rims, and even the slight turned up corners of his lips, seemed to say God had allowed this dreamer a wonderful life of adventure.

The other Billy Joe, too, was on his last days on earth. The cocked hat pulled in its many odd positions had been explained to me as I had visited him recently. I had finally asked him why it was often a-kilter. He smiled and then coughing, laughed, "Oh that? I just had a system. If it was placed at 90 degrees, it meant to shut off the water to the cows. If it was off at ten o'clock, it meant call the banker. If it was on backwards, it meant to pick up Esther Mae in the back quarter for lunch." As we looked out over his pasture with the cows grazing in belly-deep grass, punctuated by an occasional yucca plant, this dreamer, too, said, "God has allowed me to have a wonderful life. I have a gorgeous wife and family, and just look at that scene there. No painting could look so perfect. Aren't they beautiful?"

Jake and the Shrink

It is sometimes asked, "Why do bad things happen to good people?" This can be turned into "Why do some people have all the bad luck?" When selecting a puppy, there is a significant amount of uncertainty about this potential member of the family. The dog's intelligence, behavior, bonding, and athletic abilities may be considerations, while phobias and fear of storms or loud noises might not even on the radar. When seeing a litter of roly-poly six-week-old puppies at your feet and hearing the plea, "Daddy can we have one?" it is easy to lose all judgment and common sense of why a family shouldn't take on another mouth to feed.

Jake was a dog whose shortcomings had been overlooked when he was adopted. When asked what I thought an animal should be named, I many times said, "Lucky," for lucky this animal found your home. Jake was one of those dogs. I'm sure he was a cute, irresistible, cuddly, squirming, puppy in perpetual motion when he originally came to the Hays family. As part of the examination of any dog, I would seriously ask, "Is your dog smart?" This could get a variety of responses such as, "He's dumber than a box of rocks, but we love him," or "She's smarter than we are," or "He doesn't have a clue," or even "How do you know?"

Jake was an English springer spaniel. His pedigree had to be stellar because they threw away the mold when he was made. He would eat any and everything. Kid's toys, food off the table, plastic, shoes, magazines, or chocolate with the wrapper; nothing was safe, and he could not be left alone in a house full of temptation.

If that was not enough, he was also deftly afraid of storms. Thunder and lightning would send him over the edge. No bed was low enough to the floor that he could not get under it. He could hear thunder in the next county. A sprinkle could fall thirty miles away, and Jake would begin to whine and pace.

This dog needed a "shrink," but the best his owners could do was me. "Why me?" would be my thought when this malcontent would come in with his spectrum of maladies. Jake was nervous about car rides. He would pant, slobber everywhere with anxiety, and spot every moving object out the window. He would whine and pull the master of the house while on his leash. He had no manners, and it was a calamity when he crossed the threshold at the vet clinic. He was always immediately escorted to an open examination room, with the door shut quickly behind him and Larry Hays. Larry was always dressed in a suit and tie and headed for work when blessed to bring Jake for his nest session with his "shrink."

"Oh, Mr. Jake, how are you this morning? What is this red stuff all over your face?" was my first observation as I slid the door open to the room. I didn't mention that Jake was also a chicken. So brave and brazen to pull Larry's arm out of the socket while tugging him on a leash, but in the vet's office, he would crawl under the chair as though asking, "You can't see me, can you?" Shoe horning him out could take three people, but once on the stainless steel elevated exam table, he became a pussycat. His body chemistry was such that he never gained weight. His long spaniel hair lay close to his body so that his ribs were very prominent, and his flanks caved in like he had been on a month long fast.

"He may have gotten into something last night" was Larry's only clue. "If it wouldn't be too much of a problem, could I leave him with you today as I'm late for work?"

"Sure. Let me just give him a quick physical while you are here, and you can be on your way," I said. I had repeated this routine many times with this pair. With Jake, if it wasn't coming out the back end in the form of a string, sock, or glove, and he wasn't upchucking candy wrappers, there were often no other symptoms.

"Well, there doesn't seem to be anything obvious, so why don't you run on to work," I said as phone numbers were checked and Larry was given a roller brush to remove the clingy hair decorating his suit coat.

Jake was put into a run for observation. About two hours later, he started to howl and nervously pace from the front to the back of the dog run. He grabbed the front gate with his teeth and shook it as if to say, "Get me out of here!" Even for Jake, this was not normal behavior while staying with us for the day. Becky, the technician, went in to hold him and console his nervous body. This was a temporary solution, for the fear and fright in his remained in his eyes. Finally, I heard it outside. A thunderstorm had blown up, and the faint distant booming could be heard. Acepromazine is a tranquilizer given for its ability to take the edge off the nervous system. Jake could have become an addict as some small pill or five drops injected under his skin would have him sleeping like a baby in minutes. Thus was the case today. Jake curled up on a mat and slept the day away.

When Larry picked him up at the closing time, the only report I could tell him was that Jake had a rough day with the storm that had blown through. However, the yellow candy or Ace had made for a very comforting leisure day for him. A small supply of Ace was sent home to be given at times of anxiety or storm phobias.

Larry had a purple Corvette. In fact, his nickname was "Purple" because of his undying loyalty to his college sports team colors.

He stopped in the office to visit about Jake about two weeks later. Larry had left Jake in the garage for the day while at work. The sports car had been moth balled for the winter. Jake decided it was fair game and thought he would redecorate its shiny purple paint job. He had applied deep scratch marks to all four doors, the hood, and the trunk. Any other person would have given Jake the death sentence, but "Purple" was more concerned about what Jake must have been thinking when he did such a naughty deed. A new paint job could mend the Corvette. So what was my advice regarding Jake's behavior?

Episode after episode occured in the Hays household. Their two children were in school, and Larry and his wife both worked outside of the home. Did Jake need a playmate? What behavior modification desensitization could I advise for this malcontent?

Then, one day, Jake experienced a sudden change in behavior. Larry brought him in to be examined because Jake had recently been waking up at night, going to the sliding patio door, and vomiting up yellowish spit. He would then crawl back into bed with Larry and sleep the rest of the night. His appetite wasn't as good as normal. His stools were still regular, but the volume had lessened. His behavior at the vet's office was a complete metamorphosis. He was a model patient. No more "you can't see me under the chair" acts or yanking Larry around every corner in pursuit of the clinic cat.

During the physical exam, all of his vital signs were normal. His color, temperature, heart, and abdomen seemed within normal limits. He had lost weight. Even for his already thin body, this was obvious to the eye, and the scale confirmed it. I interrogated his master with questions: "No vomiting of food? Diarrhea? Are you missing anything in the house? No objects in the bowel movements? Are they the normal size and color? Does his stomach seem to growl or make noises?" I sent home a medication to cut down on the stomach acid and treat the yellow bile spit up at nights. It was to be given orally at bedtime. There didn't seem to be any reason for an X-ray as I could feel for any abdominal obstructions with my hands.

On several more trips to see me over the next six months, Jake continued to lose weight. There were no more new symptoms or signs. He hadn't taken any acepromazine for months. There were no other medications that he could have gotten into accidentally. Larry's concerns were becoming obvious. "How could this change in Jake's personality come on so suddenly?" he pondered.

"Larry, I know we have discussed this, but I believe it is time for an X-ray. We'll need to give him a light anesthetic, so he will lie perfectly still. We can then see on the film all of the organs and tissues. If there is nothing found, I'll give him some barium to watch it go through his intestinal system. I can then take some additional views of the abdomen."

"Amazing!" I exclaimed as I viewed the black and white picture on the view box. "It looks like a Ladybug! How could it be such a perfect shape in the intestine?" I stared in awe at the picture before me. I hurried back to the table to see if I could touch the object I was seeing in the X-ray. Jake was still unconscious and relaxed. "Ah ha!" there it was. Way up under the rib cage, I could just barely touch this foreign body as I pressed my fingers together from both sides of the abdomen.

I immediately called Larry at work. "Hey Purple, do I have news for you!" I happily reported. "I have a possibly found the answer to Jake's malady!"

"Okay, what do you have?" he slowly intervened.

"Are you possibly missing a metal Ladybug?" I quizzed him.

"Well, I didn't know it was missing, but, yes, I believe we do have a refrigerator magnet in the shape of a Ladybug. Why do you ask?" he mused.

"It seems that Jake must have swallowed it, and it is lodged in his duodenum. It is in a perfect silhouette on the X-ray. It must be laying in such a position that some food must be able to pass around it. That would be the reason that he is not vomiting regularly and that he was having some stools," I explained as I tried to reason the saga of the last six months.

That afternoon, the flat, three-inch diameter Ladybug was removed from Jake's intestine. He recovered from the surgery in fine fashion. Post-surgical food intake and normal bowel movements were perfect. Aside from a newly ravenous appetite, reconvening his nervous howling, and his continued penchant for eating anything that was not nailed down, Jake had made a complete recovery. The surgeon could rest, but his "shrink" would be called back onto duty.

Beg'er Pardon

America came to love the cowboy through movies and television. The real cowboys were just wranglers who surely did not all wear guns, black or white hats, or spend glamorous time in saloons or street show-downs with a bad guy or clan. Real American cowboys were spread over cattle country from Texas to Montana and all places in between. Making a living raising cattle involved lean times, meager wages, and stormy weather. The niceties of a clean bed, ironed shirts, new boots, three "squares," and close knit family units did not depict the life that they lived. Roundups, cattle drives, roping and branding scenes are Technicolor imaginations.

A television series in the 1950s and 1960s called *Wagon Train* was the first prime time western series that involved a wagon master and his crew helping pioneers and settlers traverse the plains and mountains heading west to California and Oregon. Some will remember the characters of Major Seth Adams as the wagon master and Flint McCullough as the scout riding his distinctive Appaloosa horse. For eight years, this hour-long series had no less than 1,417 actors and actress during its 320 episodes. This who's who list of Hollywood greats would include a future president and first lady, popular rock and roll stars, and every cowboy star to ever hit the screen. I mention these famous guest stars to demonstrate the magnitude of *Wagon Train's* influence on the American culture at the time. Flint McCullough's appaloosa horse was the most notable animal on the screen. Cowboys in the movies all rode solid color horses like sorrels, blacks, palominos, and bays.

Flint's horse with its white-blanketed rump was the most colorful regular on the set.

The Appaloosa became a fad, and the numbers across the country multiplied with this popularity. Appaloosa horse clubs and breeding stallions standing at stud promoted this breed. With such rapid demand, these breeders often did not discriminate or select for all genetic traits. Merely breeding for a white blanket or frosted spots does not always take into account confirmation, size, agility, or even intelligence. This is not the best way to select for color, and as a result, low intelligence and less than desirable confirmation became the trademark of the breed.

With movie stars, western sunsets, and the image of the scout galloping away from the Conestogas in my mind, I soon had the real life cowboy and the Appaloosa's popularity standing before me.

Early one March morning, a wiry cowboy appeared at the counter. Willis McCann introduced himself and began to ramble about his foaling problems at Beaver Lake Stables. His hat was perfectly trained and shaped, with a small feather accenting the sweat stained brim cocked back in a manner of importance. His stud snapped plaid shirt accentuated his slim torso. A big embossed belt buckle cinched his khakis, the pleated legs neatly tucked into his bright patterned boots. He seemed to have a hearing problem, but a quick survey showed no noticeable hearing aids. Through his wire rims he reminded me of Festus on *Gun Smoke*. He responded to my questions with a habitual "Beg'er pardon" comeback to things that he either did not hear or statements that he did not want to hear.

"So Willis, how many foals do you have?" I asked.

"Beg'er pardon?" he returned.

I repeated and tried to talk louder, enunciating the words while facing him directly. "What are the problems you are having?" my lips worked to present the words with perfect diction without letting on that I sensed his hearing problem.

"Well Doc, I have lost two, and two more are weak. They have watery poop," he casually stated. "Could you come out to see what is killing them? They are worth a lot, and I just can't seem to figure it out. They are the highest priced Appaloosas in the Midwest," he added, thinking that I would be impressed.

No way! How could I be so lucky? The few recent backyard Appaloosas that I had worked on were fat, lazy, and not the brightest. They would act like knuckleheads when I tried to examine them, by stepping on your feet and acting flighty. They were, in general, a pain.

"Big hat, no cattle!" is a common phrase to designate those cowboys who may dress the part but don't have any cattle and don't know much about them. This was the picture I had of Willis McCann.

So it was out to the Appaloosas and Beaver Lake Stables with Little Red sloshing through the mud holes in the lane leading to the ranch house. Aiming down a steep, icy hill with moguls, Red slid into the low bungalow shed and paddock. This white painted cinder block building looked more like a low dugout with a tin thatched overhanging roof than a stable. Upwards of twenty Appaloosas were stalled in individual pens. Each pen was divided with neatly welded sucker rods. These inside pens stood out as unusually excellent quality, quite different from the outside appearance of the stable housing. Inside the construction, it was very cold and damp with no air movement or ventilation fans. Condensation on the metal roof occasionally formed large droplets that splatted like distant artillery charges when coursing the alleyway. The alleys were lined with a calcium carbonate powder to help dry them which provided clean, good footing for the farmhand or cowboy stable helper. Fluorescent light tubes that hung overhead had seen many hours and produced a dimmed yellowish hue.

I did a quick surveillance, taking in the conditions and the horses that had all come to attention as a stranger had come into the barn. As with any examination, there were many questions. "Beg'er pardon" was the first response, but repeating the same questions louder and slower led me to believe that Willis had heard me the first time and was using this phrase as a time to come up with a good answer. The questioning and history of the stable management and the foal deaths proceeded slowly.

These babies had a bacterial dysentery which would respond well to treatment if they could be rehydrated and warmed to revive them from their near comatose condition. With Willis's help, we cradled one wet little dappled foal into a hand-me-down fleece blanket and tucked her limp body into Little Red's front passenger seat for a return trip to the clinic. With the heater on full blast and the foggy windows from this added soaked body, we pulled ourselves back up the slouchy driveway. I radioed for Cali to have a mattress and hot water bottles ready. "And would you have some fluids and IV materials ready as there won't be much time to spare to save this foal?"

Intravenous therapy can be tricky — a lactated ringer's solution cannot be given too fast or it will overwhelm the blood volume, as it is osmometrically absorbed into the tissue cells. As such, adding potassium and bicarbonate to balance the blood's pH becomes a challenge for the technician to monitor regularly. An antibiotic in the IV and penicillin in the back leg muscle helped slow the bacterial assault. The angry and inflamed intestine responded well, and this little filly was miraculously ready to go home late in the afternoon.

Willis wheeled into the upper lot at about closing time. The scrawny little filly was loaded into his Bronco wagon. I cradled her during the drive to prevent her from getting up–she was all legs, and was ready to run. I held her in the vinyl seats, and Cali followed in Little Red to pick me up and bring me back to the office. With country western songs blaring on the radio, we bounced out to the stables. Willis did not hear anything as I responded to his rapid fire questions. His smile and gratitude was somewhat muffled by the fact that he may not have known how close this little filly was to dying.

Her huge 1,500 pound marble colored momma nickered continually when we crossed the threshold with her now bright and beautiful baby. She threw back her ears as we approached her stall as if to say, "Where have you been with my baby?" It was my hope that in this well straw-bedded stall, she would be able to stay dry. I handed Willis the tube of probiotics and antibiotic paste to administer by mouth at six-hour intervals. Confident that he understood the directions, I turned and walked down the darkened alleyway to leave as the stinging damp wind hit my face in the paddock outside. Taking a deep breath and shaking my head, I hoped for a weather turn so that these paddocks would dry soon and the horses could be turned out into the sun and green grass. Sunlight and dry green pastures are better that any medicines in a bottle.

Several more calls to Beaver Lake Stables in the ensuing months were complicated by spring flooding and mud and water in the stables. I have to admit that the Appaloosas were quite a beautiful sight in the green pasture as I saw them on my trips through the countryside. Flint McCullough would have thought this was a *Wagon Train* setting. Losing foals and having chronic respiratory problems seemed to be a constant problem for Willis despite my attempts to train him on preventative procedures, health, and nutrition alternatives.

Late on a Friday afternoon in June, after several weeks of not hearing from him, the phone message alerted me of colic at the ranch. A colic at this time of the day could lead to a long evening of treatments and walking, or it could be a quick intravenous injection of an analgesic and anti-spasmodic. I remembered that we had family plans to go to the Waterloo Community Playhouse musical that night with my wife and girls. Because we had these tickets, I assumed that this was going to be a difficult and protracted colic. With the grasshoppers spreading the way as Little Red descended into the now rough, dry, rutted driveway toward the paddock, I could see the leopard colored stallion lying down, rolling, and then suddenly jumping up. His sweaty dust covered coat showed he'd been repeating this process for a while and that the pain from the colic was intense.

Willis met me at the gate as I reached into the vet box for my grip. I grimly announced to him, "It doesn't look good." I had used these four words many times to a farmer or pet owner as my first appraisal of their animal's prospects. The thready rapid pulse through the stethoscope confirmed my visual analysis. A normal horse heart sounds low and gives off a unique rhythmic lub-dub. Normally a horse's heart rate is around sixteen beats per minute, but with pain the frequency of the beats and the crisp opening and closing of the heart valves quickly exude a staccato pitter patting. The conjunctiva of the inner eyelid was beet red and the pink mucosa of the lips and gum line above the front teeth showed very poor capillary refill time when I pressed with my thumb. As fiery red as the conjunctiva was, the gums were a contrasting muddy blue.

A listen to the abdomen revealed no normal borborygma sounds or noises indicating any movement of the intestine. All this time, Charger, as he was known, seemed oblivious to my presence and the examinations as the painful spasms hit him in lightning impulse waves. I had to finish the examination as I coaxed Willis to walk him with the lead rope tugging at his halter. As I reached the underside of his belly, I noticed the scrotum and prepuce were more swollen and puffy than I had ever seen. I slid on a rubber obstetric sleeve, and lubricated it with KY Jelly and entered the anal opening and rectum to probe the colon. I was barely into the pelvic inlet when I touched the cause of Charger's demise. A loop of the small intestine had become strangulated and descended into the inguinal ring going down into the scrotum with the testicle. I tried gentle tension on the bowel but it was stuck and swollen beyond any retraction.

"Willis, I have found the problem, and it is not good," I tried to explain. My face should have shown the hopelessness of the situation at hand. The only hope to save Charger was surgery at the equine hospital at Iowa State Vet College some two hours away. I knew the surgery would be expensive and that my bills had lingered long— Willis's ability to pay even me was not good.

I administered an IV for some pain relief, but it did not seem to dull the extreme sensation of the intestinal herniation. Putting the huge stallion to sleep when only a few hours before he had been proudly pacing the pasture was a tragic thought. When explaining that even a $5,000 surgical procedure would be the only thing that could save his life, I did my best to assure Willis that even with surgery, Charger may not make it due to the length of time the strangulation had been going on. This delicate handling of the final decision was done over a painstaking half hour when time was of the essence.

I gave Charger another dose of Banamine and helped wedge him onto the two-horse trailer. He and Willis headed up and out of the steep and bouncy driveway, the taillights blurred with dust. The sun was setting as they departed for Ames. I had called ahead to the university emergency service, and the equine surgeon called back shortly. I knew it was an "it doesn't look good" moment but wanted him to know ahead of the arrival and my assessment and drugs that I had given. I asked that he call me with the outcome after he had a chance to see Willis and his headstrong, suffering stallion. By this time, any thoughts of a musical play had long passed. I radioed home to tell Cynthia of the circumstances. This night and through the next forty years of practice, I had her loving understanding. She never wavered in her concern and beliefs that the animal needed me more. A veterinarian's spouse has to take the same subconscious oath that we take to relieve pain and suffering not to mention the "for better or worse" part.

Two hours passed when I got a call at about midnight at my bedside phone. Charger had been put to sleep. He had struggled during the two-hour drive to the surgeon, and they were not able to get him to rise in the trailer.

The answer to why these things happen is always the most difficult part of medicine. Beaver Lake Stables and my friend "Beg'er Pardon" Willis sure seemed to have more than their share of bad luck.

Birds of a Feather

As a young farm boy, my all-time favorite day of February was going to the post office to pick up the delivery of baby chicks. The cacophonic cheeping of these two hundred one-day-old little fluffy chicks reverberated from behind the rows of upright mailboxes. A faint sweet smell of pressed straw mesh bedding filled the air. Two cardboard boxes divided into quarters each held one hundred cheepers. These little Rhode Island Reds had been hatched the day before in a Kansas City hatchery. Then they were boxed and shipped by mail to reach us some three hundred miles west by the next day.

My dad must have loved this event too. Though he never showed his excitement outwardly, he had prepared a warm welcome for them. The brooder house was waiting for them on their arrival at the farmstead. This small hut with two windows and a door had in its center a drop down galvanized natural gas-heated brooder. The chicks were placed under the now-warm hovering tent with the temperature set at one hundred degrees. Small openings on the quadrangular flaps allowed the chicks to dart in and out to eat, drink, and exercise. They played and frolicked like any other young animal whether they were calves, foals, piglets, or puppies, scattering the chopped corncob bedding, standard absorbing litter, under the brooder and surrounding wooden lathe floor. It would be this experience and memory of these baby chicks with their continual cheeping and playing that gave me a love for chickens.

Cleaning out the chicken house somehow became my job. I would shovel the bedding and chicken droppings into my red racer wagon, which would then be pulled to the cornfield where it would be spread for fertilizer. One day, an enterprising idea came to my Tom Sawyer mind that this chicken manure surely must have some value. Eliciting the help of the neighbor Gosselin boys, we set off for town with our three wagons filled with the chicken dropping to be sold as fertilizer. What seemed like a great idea became a downer as even three little boys' begging met deaf ears. We had no luck persuading housewives of the value of chicken manure for their gardens. At twenty-five cents per load, it sure seemed like a bargain to us. Finally, the banker's wife couldn't resist our innocent endeavors and bought all of our supply—three wagons full for twenty-five cents.

Fifteen years later in veterinary school, the sounds of peeping chickens became "fifteen love...thirty love...forty love" as a yellow felt Wilson lobbed back and forth over the net. Dr. West's infamous "Chicken Medicine" class as we dubbed it, was formally known as Avian Medicine. Dr. West was a noted birdman whose knowledge of avian pathology was renowned. However, his lectures were exhaustingly boring and would have put Rip Van Winkle back to sleep. Whether it was air sacculitis, enlarged livers, petechial hemorrhages, mucous discharge, watery stool, ruffled feathers, every disease seemed to have the same signs. The slow, monotonous, soft delivery could overcome any amount of caffeine stimulant. Trading our talents to a more physical challenge, four of us, Broadway Joe Pavilik, Pursley, Bartlett, and myself, would sneak out the side door for our twice-weekly tennis match. Gone were any ideas of trying to memorize the difference between avian influenza, New Castle's Disease, or Salmonella enteritis. I just knew I would never need to know any more about chickens or any feathered fowl in my veterinary career.

Practice would prove differently, as I was continually challenged with turkeys, swans, caged pet birds, and backyard chicken operations. Roger Heise was a John Deere engineer and lived on a small acreage hobby farm. He and his wife, Alice, had a penchant for the unusual. They were born under the sign of Aquarius, on the same date, though one year apart. They had been childhood sweethearts and had been married fifty years. Together, their humor and love for animals of all kinds gave me an opportunity for the extraordinary. They had a beef herd, several nice quarter horses, a handful of ponies, and, of course, some free range chickens.

The Heises' chicken coop was filled with every imaginable breed and color of squawkers. If it weren't for their ability to fend off predators of all makes and kinds, their numbers would have been nil. Soaring hawks in the morning hours, ravenous skunks during the afternoons, and raccoons at nights each required their own defenses. Finding a hawk with a chicken in its claws, a skunk sucking the blood out of another, or the malicious killing by raccoons made for many adventures for the barnyard free rangers. The smartest of the chicken breeds are the Bantams or Banties. At the bottom of the "pecking order" for brains are the white Leghorns. Leghorns have no clue of impending danger, whereas Bantams are constantly surveying the air for a diving kamikaze chicken hawk.

Little Peep was a Sebring Bantam who had been hatched in the farm incubator. This yellow fuzz ball had almost drowned as a chick when an upright water jar fell and pinned her underneath. Soaked, chilled, and in shock from her nighttime accident, she was rescued by Alice the next morning. This lifeless little handful was brought into the house and dried with a hand held hair dryer. With her eyes still closed she made a faint response, "Peep…Peep," and then another "Peep." Oh, Alice was thrilled to see that there was life! "Come on Little Peep, you can do it," she coaxed.

Thus, the name Little Peep. As she matured, first losing her downy chick hair, then pin feathers of adolescence, and finally acquiring her beautiful, teal, crimson, and gold adult feathers, she emerged into a beautiful poult. She really thought she was a human— she bonded with Roger and Alice like their adopted hen-child.

Little Peep, now full grown, became Roger's favorite hen. She rode on the tractor with him, sitting on the fender and acting as navigator. Her attention was directed toward the surrounding fieldwork. She would turn her head sideways when Roger would talk to her as though she understood and found his vocalization stimulating. She would follow him everywhere he went around the farm, running behind to stay in step with his movements. When not with him, she would squat on the front steps and wait for him to come home from work.

She followed them like a puppy as they did their chores of feeding the cattle, horses, and gathering the eggs in the hen house. She rocked her head, as if she understood everything the Heises said to her. She even greeted all that came to the farm. Little Peep greeted the roofers that were hired to replace the shingles on the older farm home. She would climb the ladder as it propped against the side of the house to peer over the roof edge as they methodically placed each tile. She would climb into the open door of their work van and hop up into the seat for a comfortable spot to observe their work as if she were the foreman.

Iowa has several statewide marquee events each summer: the renowned Iowa State Fair, RAGBRAI, or the Register's Annual Great Bike Ride across Iowa, and the Tractor Ride. The Tractor Ride traverses the back country roads as five hundred tractors meander and putter along on a three-day adventure. It was on this Tractor Ride that Little Peep nearly met her Waterloo, as this particular year's Tractor Cade just happened to be from Sheffield to Waterloo, Iowa, covering a distance of eighty miles.

Roger and Alice diligently cleaned and polished their John Deere 30 while Little Peep watched with intrigue. With her head nodding and observing first with one eye and then the next, she clucked and seemed to know this was not the usual trip to the field to cultivate corn. When a bright yellow carpet remnant was velcroed onto the fender, she immediately took up squatter rights. This tractor was going nowhere without Little Peep.

Every size, shape, age, and color of these engines chugged out on the blacktop in the dawn light. Big ones, little ones, canopy topped, and antiques, this conclave of engines emerged like water bugs on a stagnant pond. Never before had a chicken been given such a ride. She perched proudly on the right fender decked out in her yellow and green John Deere bandana. Little Peep was the celebrity of the year, but she acted like it was just the normal routine — it was nothing to squawk about!

The June heat and humidity on this three-day tractor trek had taken its toll on some of the less seasoned tractors and riders. Meandering over long distances on hard surface is not the normal torque and work load for these powerhouses. At frequent stops and starts at roadside stands and concessionaires, Little Peep sat high, taking in the spectacle. Bystanders oohed and aahed as they passed, taking off their sunglasses to make sure they were really seeing this chic chick. Mary's little lamb at school could not have caused such a commotion.

At the end of the third day on this exhausting journey, little Peep was tired. All day as they had passed fence rows, waterways, pastures, and corn fields, the heat was taking its measure on this brave little pullet. That night as the Heises camped, the charcoal smoked as the shadows descended on the rolling hills. Little Peep just rested in a squatting position, occasionally straining and making a slight painful grunting noise. Sensing that things were not just right, Roger filled an empty gallon milk jug with warm water. He placed it in Little Peep's crate to keep her warm and tucked her in for the night. During the night, a pin hole leak in the plastic jug started; and it soaked the towel under her bed. It wicked up her feathers, drenching her like a string sailor's mop. At the break of dawn, she laid motionless and shivered sporadically. The hair dryer was used again to try to revive her. It was moved back and forth under each layer of feathers spraying a mist as it blew warm air through the tunnels and feather shafts. Slowly her eyes opened, but a third eyelid membrane remained over the lower cornea. For the time being, she had made roll call.

When the engines started to their putt putt morning rhythm, there was no Little Peep perched on her yellow pad as the tractors "pulled out of Dodge." She remained in the camper to ride with the chase vehicle until she was feeling better. Stopping for a lunch break at a church stand with its assortment of sandwiches and potato salads, the tractor and Roger came to a rest. There under a tree in the shade, Alice and Little Peep joined him for a picnic. Peep was still depressed and only opened her eyes slightly as she recognized her master's voice. "It will be okay little girl. We'll be home tonight and get out of this heat," he affectionately told her, petting her with each slowly drawled word.

"Doc, I've got a problem," came the call that night. While these words were to be repeated on phone calls on a daily occurrence, this distress call from Roger was unusual. His voice was soft and cracked a few times as he replayed the events of the last week. I listened intently, trying to understand the whole episode of tractors, heat, food stands, leaking water jugs, and picnics. I sensed an underlying tone that Little Peep was in trouble.

"Sure, Roger, I can meet you at the office tonight. No problem," I responded. Had the stress been too much for this little chicken to endure? Had she caught the chills from the water soaking? Had she become dehydrated from the heat? These and other possibilities swam in my mind as I pulled on my boots. I sped off to the office to aid my friend and his sick chick.

"Well, Roger, you are right. She sure looks punk!" I paused to observe the little shivering hen on the table. "Has she been eating or drinking since she started your journey?" I questioned, trying to understand why this little bird was sitting motionless on the mat on the exam table. Sure, it was nighttime and long past Little Peep's roosting time, but this was not how this little character should have been acting as I passed the penlight into her eyes.

"You know, I can't tell you the last time I saw her drink any water," Roger mumbled back to my question.

That was it! The lights in my head flashed, and I sensed that this might be the problem. Was she dehydrated? I'd never heard of this before. Grasping at straws, there it was bigger than life. I looked at Little Peep's bottom side. Her vent was swollen and pink. Could she be so dehydrated that she had not enough moisture or mucous to properly lubricate the egg in her oviduct? A thick egg white discharge was coming from the opening.

"Roger, this may sound crazy, but I believe that this may be part of the problem," I claimed as I parted the feathers to show him the inflamed and swollen bottom. "I believe she is egg bound!"

"Never heard of it, but if you say so, what the heck do we do now?" Roger hopefully asked.

"Sure enough, there it is. Wow, is that huge. No wonder she's hurting," I said in amazement as I viewed the X-ray film showing the egg lodged just inside the vent opening.

With some lubricant on my finger and a syringe of soapy water, I irrigated the periphery and injected some of the solution into the oviduct. Applying some pressure around the circumference, out slowly popped the huge speckled egg. Little Peep slowly stood up as if to say, "Oh, what a relief it is!" Her eyes opened completely for the first time. Her whole body shook twice and she flapped her wings as if to say, "Let's get out of here."

Never had I known such an intelligent animal as Little Peep. Climbing ladders, riding tractors, welcoming visitors, and now this egg bound episode. She was truly one of a kind. I recalled a wise veterinary instructor who had said to the class at the end of a lecture, "You will never get rich as a veterinarian, but you surely will see a wonderful rich variety!" What a profound statement it was. This Little Peep was a special variety.

Honey, Cowboy, and a Spanish Star Fire

What's in a name? One sweet, one a wholesome all around nice guy, and one rebellious; these three names happened to be the orneriest trio of broncs I ever met along the trail.

The love a little girl can form for a horse is a precious and inexplicable thing. How can a small eighty-pound ten-year-old be drawn to a large powerful steed some fifteen times her weight? Little girls can communicate with a horse like no other human. Seeing them with their arms draped around an elongated head and nose, hugging and caressing an understanding horse is a sight that happens all around the globe. Though some may be afraid to ride or even sit on the back of the horse at first, with a brush in hand a girl builds confidence, and cements a relationship with the horse that eliminates all fears.

I had this same love for my own horse, Babe. As an adolescent, this powerful horse would glide below me with graceful symmetry. I rode bareback, only holding onto the reins, galloping to nowhere in particular, with the wind in my young face. My eyes would water and run down my cheeks as my grin stretched from ear to ear. The rhythmic thudding of hooves made each step vibrate through the whole body, giving a magical feeling of oneness between a boy and his horse. Patting the sweaty neck and talking love to a snorting half-ton animal brought freedom and peace from all of the other outside problems in a farm boy's life. A horse's head and neck is incredibly strong, yet with a gentle touch of the rein and a bit in its mouth, it turns and eases forward with grace.

Little girls grow up to get metallic braces on their own teeth. Boys and other interests such as sports and cars come into their lives and vie for their love, yet time with a horse overcomes all other loves. Nothing compares to the sweaty saddle blanket smell, the cinch flopping as the saddle is lugged from the framed storage perch, or the bridle as the bit slides into the horse's mouth. When girls become strong enough to tug and throw the saddle up onto their four legged companion's back, they become truly free of any distractions—no boy or car could even compete for their affection.

Honey, Cowboy, and Star came into my life after I was introduced to Herb Wydert's barn and Kerr Stables—two locations within the city limits of our towns that stabled horses for horse-loving pre-teens and their grown-up counterparts. Honey may sound sweet, and she was in the hands of little Jenny, but when the vet in the blue coverall medical suit would arrive, her nose would immediately flare and she'd start to snort. Her eyes would bulge, and she would start dancing. Her fear and nervous prancing made indicated she was not going to be an easy horse to inoculate or do a teeth check. Sure enough, even with Herb's firm grip as he coaxed her into the stocks, she was defiant to any touch or cajoling talk. Honey would break into a coat–drenching sweat, and would surely have loved to plant her front hoof right between my eyes if given the chance. Calling her Honey as I petted her and tried to reassure her was as effective as talking to a brick wall. This scene would never improve during her lifetime.

Little girls inevitably grow up go to college and move away from home, which makes it difficult to keep their horses. Some of them outgrow their smaller horse, and another companion horse draws their attention and time. Such an occurrence happened with Honey's—when her little girl grew, Honey moved from the stable to another little girl on a new farm where she was the only horse. I was called in the spring to vaccinate a horse for a young family. They lived on Bennington Road north of town out in the country. At the end of a winding driveway lined with newly planted, rope supported maples, a red barn and white fence came into view. A ten-year-old girl in a cowboy hat and boots waited with her mother as Little Red came to rest. Much to my horror, I spied their dear sweet Honey galloping around the small dry lot paddock, snorting and kicking up her heels. The girl's mother was surprised by these actions. Honey had been so docile and obedient for them— this behavior was quite alien. Honey was captured and tied to a freshly painted wooden fence post in the dry lot so the vaccination procedures could be accomplished. No blood, no stepped on feet, no twitch or hand full of ear was needed. To say that I had some horse sense would be appropriate, but Honey did try my patience. With little girls, she was like butter on bread, but with the vet, she would rather have seen me dead.

***

Cowboy was a black and white horse whose color resembled a Dutch belted cow, or possibly a skunk. Never could a horse have been named so appropriately—his personality waivered in a very Jekyll and Hyde way. His fear of a stranger was much different than Honey's. He would bare his teeth like a cornered dog. His coat was heavy year–round; when aggravated, it would come out in clumps like a shedding malamute. Spitting floating hair and dust particles became the norm when working with him. It was like his nerve ending to his skin would release his hair follicles as a defensive dust screen when the vet arrived. Rachel was his soul mate.

"Hi Rachel. I am Dr. Kenyon," I greeted her as I peered into the stable front door. "Is this your horse?" The youngster stood high on the rung of the stall door in her cowboy hat and boots, decked out with skintight Wranglers and a T-shirt. Her cheerleader physique seemed a contradiction to the blocky, stalky body of this Cowboy friend of hers.

"Yes, he is," she timidly replied.

"Well, do you think you could catch him, or do you want me to help?" I clinched my teeth in anticipation.

"You know he really is not like this with me," Rachel said apologetically as she stared worryingly at this now pawing malcontent.

"Wow. You know, Rachel, how about if I get back in my truck and drive out of the yard. You can try to catch him and lead him out of the barn. I will meet you over there on the grass next to that old oak tree." I begged for a solution to the stalemate with this cantankerous critter.

Rachel happily agreed to this game plan with her Cowboy. I had no real purpose for all these directives but knew there was no way I wanted any part in Cowboy's teeth bearing antics while trying to catch him in his stall.

Since there were no other adults around, this change in venue would have to work for now.

I drove out of the barnyard. After a few minutes, I emerged from my now hidden red pickup truck. There, pleasantly eating grass under the burr oak was the docile old plug with his adoring mighty mite nonchalantly holding the end of the dangling lead rope.

I had taken off the blue jump suit, shed the baseball cap, and donned my straw cowboy hat from the truck. Whistling my way along the pealing white fence board, I jumped over to approach the scene of the action. The morning light shimmered on the dew droplets and penetrated the foggy haze. Having no idea what this barrel chested knucklehead would think of the change of venue, I approached cautiously. I happily greeted Rachel and Cowboy like I had never seen them before. With Cowboy's green stained muzzle chewing contently on the lush orchard grass, I knew working on his teeth was out of the question for today's primetime event.

"Okay, big guy. So they call you Cowboy, huh?" I bravely offered small talk. "So, you just need a little four-way sleeping sickness and tetanus shot today?" I kept expecting him to bolt, or turn up his lip with suspicion. I rubbed the bridge of his nose as he nuzzled his brawny head into me asking for more petting. Was this the same horse I had just witnessed a few minutes earlier that would have kicked me six feet under?

Keeping one hand across his nose, I carefully removed the syringe of pink vaccine from my back pocket. Never letting Cowboy's eyes see what was coming his way, I thumped his chest three times with the back of my hand. On the fourth thump, the needle was thrust deeply into the pectoral muscles. In a flash, the inoculation was done. Cowboy's only complaint was that he wanted to drop his head for another bite of grass.

Little Rachel had no clue that this was not the normal behavior of her horse. I thought, *No guts, no glory!* "Okay, Cowboy, I'm done with you for now. Happy trails to you and Rachel," I said as I turned to make my exit back over the fence. I didn't want to overstay my welcome. I would not have another chance to make a good first impression with this horse. I would eventually need to make another visit to work on Cowboy's teeth or to treat a wire cut or injury. The last experience is what a horse will always remember. Whistling as I jauntily walked away, I had a satisfying feeling of conquering a mountain and was off to the next challenge.

***

Spanish Star Fire was a light brown Buckskin with a dark two-inch stripe running from her withers to the base of her tail. She lived at Hide Away Acres, a remote acreage nestled behind a grove of hardwoods. The small and tidy cookie cutter barn with two stalls opened out into several wooden fence-lined paddocks. This quaint vista was the home of Fred and Betty Hoffman. Their daughter's wish for a horse had led them to this rural dream home.

Star had come to them as a two-year-old filly. She was spoiled with carrots, apples, and candy, and doted on with brushings, petting, and grooming. Manners were not her strong point. If she wanted to bolt and run, off she flew. When she didn't want to be caught, a posse would have no chance to corner her. When she didn't want a bridle or saddle placed on her back, it took an hour of cajoling to accomplish the act. I would not say that she was over loved, but would settle for "She had never been properly trained."

Laurie was a pretty girl who had no idea of some of the antics that a horse on a long lead rope in a small stall may produce. Being stepped on, head butted, rump squeezed against the wall by her youthful filly was not uncommon. It was not in my manner to send a horse to "boot camp" for a month, but Star would have been a candidate at the top of the list. Somehow the Hoffmans were able to break her to ride with the help of a neighboring horse man. She tolerated these jaunts around the adjoining gravel roads. She was not very tuned to the beauty of nature around her or the unity of her rider sitting high in a stiff, newly minted saddle on her rounded back. Walking, clippity-clopping along was her preferred gait. For Laurie and her father, this was also the safest speed. Star would seldom break into a sweat on these short forays along Buckridge. She would whinny and greet the other backyard, seldom ridden mounts living a suburban lifestyle on their small backwoods acreages. These overfed pets would run along their fence lines, prancing like they were getting ready for the Derby. This was the most exercise some of them would see in a week. On the return trip home, Star would be pumped and could even be encouraged to a slow gallop as she made the mad sprint back home. This was an everyday occurrence. Simply holding on with both hands, stirrups flying, was the best defense positioning her rider could muster. Star had no intention of throwing her rider or bucking in this dash, she only wanted to get home to her tidy little barn and the couch potato lifestyle of carrots, apples, and candy.

A farrier and veterinarian would be the only outside visitors that Star would ever encounter. Having her nose twitched or someone pulling down hard with a hand wrapped around her ear was new for this softy. This made an examination, a vaccination, or any foot work tolerable for me. Only once was there a minor injury, which occurred when Laurie got tangled in the lead rope, was stepped on, and broke her ankle.

Laurie grew up and left for college and later a job. She left her Star behind in a setting that she expected to never change.

The idea was hatched around a holiday dinner table. Star was lonely. She needed another horse to keep her company. She needed a baby. With her bloodlines, it would be a shame not to pass on her genetics. This beautiful Buckskin must be mated with a stallion that would match her beauty.

"Hi, Dr. Jim. This is Laurie Hoffman. I'm home for the holidays," she gleefully informed me.

"Oh hello. Welcome home. How can I help you?" I curiously anticipated the reason for her call.

"Well, it's about Star. We would like her to have a foal and want you to come out to see her and tell us if it would be possible for her to get pregnant," she asked enthusiastically.

My head pressing moment ensued with hand to the forehead and the elbow planted on the desk. Shaking my head back and forth, I said, "Sure I can come out. Have the coffee pot on, and we'll visit about the particulars for Star."

Upon arriving at Hide Away Acres, I was greeted warmly by the three Hoffmans and ushered to the kitchen island to an awaiting stool. Black freshly roasted coffee warmed my hands in none other than a horse-monogramed mug with a handle shaped like a horse's tail. A richly buttered cinnamon roll melted in my mouth as I peered out the sliding glass door to see Star with a winter blanket strapped around her. She was rummaging through her hay, seeming most content in her penthouse arrangement on the farm. I sat down for the upcoming reproductive discussion. After some time visiting about a vacation, the new job, and the boyfriend, I prepared myself for the proposal.

"So Jim," Laurie started, "we've been thinking that Star is depressed. We think she needs a companion now that I don't see her very much. You know she is now nine years old, and if she's ever going to have a baby her time may be running out." Laurie presented her case. "What do you think?"

All of a sudden, the ball was in my court. "Whoa. Wait a sec! Don't make me the deciding factor," I smiled and laughed at the Hoffmans' overture. Many thoughts of this mare with a foal raced through my mind. How would this family with a seldom ridden Star ever be able to adjust to a colt flying around the barnyard? Would the spoiled Star know how to mother and be able to share her princess lifestyle with a gangly-legged colt nudging her for nourishment? What about haltering, leading, and training another yearling when his mother had barely accomplished this act?

Grinning, I said, "Sure, I think she could have a foal without any worries." I knew I was sitting on a precarious stool. I was being steam rolled. The die had already been cast. I did not even have veto power.

"Well, here are some facts you need to know," I philosophically offered to the conversation. Mrs. Hoffman poured another cup of coffee and offered another roll. I shook my head on the roll, not wanting to stay all day. "The gestation time for a horse is eleven months. Mares are seasonally polyestrous, adjusting to the length of the day in the spring and the fall, and come into heat every three weeks. You will need to have her foal come in March or April, so you can do the math," I continued. Notes were being taken. They were all ears, so I marched on. "The time will fly by quickly, so you'll need to locate a stallion. You will take Star to the stallion because it will be his home turf, and the breeder will know how to handle all of the details. I would suggest you wait another three weeks and cover her a second time. I know some of these facts you already know, but I wanted you all to know what you are going to be faced with," I summarized. I knew this was just the tip of the iceberg of the many questions to come, but I thought this would be a framework from which to start.

I must have not been too discouraging because all three of them nodded, grinned, and beamed with anticipation. I had taken the bait, and now they knew that I was a full accomplice in this dreamy venture of a new foal frolicking through their cookie cutter pastures of Hide Away Acres. I got the sense if I stayed much longer in conversation, we would be discussing the actual foaling procedure and delivery. This would have to wait for the many more coffee sessions to come in the next year of anticipation.

Lying in my bed one evening over a year later, reading a book, I was startled as the phone jingled on the bedside table. I wondered what this call could be about, and would I need to put down my Michener book and rush off into the nippy March evening to assist in a calving or lambing?

"Hello, this is Dr. Kenyon," I welcomed. "How may I help you?"

"Jim, Jim, Jim!" Mrs. Hoffman frantically exclaimed. "We need you right now! Fred just went to check on Star, and she's laying down straining, and he sent me to call you. Laurie is off on a business trip and oh my—I can hardly talk—just come as quickly as you can," she gasped.

"No problem. I'll be right on my way," I returned, knowing it would be useless to say, "Just calm down."

My headlights bounced off the leafless woods as the pickup dodged potholes from the hard winter's remaining grasp on the country roads. A white tailed deer meandered in front of Little Red as I slowed to avoid a confrontation. Sure enough, her little band of brothers were hiding in the ditch as I stopped to allow this migration the right of way. Didn't they know I was on a mission of high priority? I honked the horn impatiently, but they only squinted and perked their ears, as they seemed stunned by the headlights. With the road clear, I rounded the corner, moved over the railroad tracks, and coasted into Hide Away Acres.

Little Red came to rest on the frost-covered grass beside the barn. Wringing his hands, Fred greeted me before I could turn off the engine. "Great, you're here in time. She's standing now and must have stopped her contractions, but she is looking around at her sides every once in a while," he continued with his description of this eventful scene.

I grabbed my stethoscope and a towel to assess the action. There was Star, more than a bit fat and wide, nibbling at her hay in the raised manger in the corner. She turned to acknowledge the arrival of a nighttime guest. Typically she would have fled outside into the paddock. She gave me a look that suggested she was too heavy with foal and running outside would take too much energy. Her thick winter coat stood on end, which only accentuated her expanded girth.

It was quite obvious to me that no foal was eminent tonight, but I could be mistaken. I listened to her heart and searched for a faint heartbeat of a foal inside her belly. The steady gurgling noises of Star's intestines growling and belching were the only noises coming through the cold stethoscope ear piece.

I was not too keen on doing a rectal exam on her, but I put on my sterile shoulder length obstetrical glove. Lubricating the surface with KY jelly, I slowly coaxed my way into Star's rectal area. Fresh, steaming green manure horse apples rushed out at this stimulation. Finally, with most of these feces emitted, I was able to ballot a fully developed fetus over the brim of the pelvis. Star groaned with the intrusion of my arm, as the fetus was already taking so much room inside her distended belly. She looked around as if to say, "Okay, you've found what you were looking for. Now please get out of my privates, and let me alone and get back to my hay!" In no more than thirty seconds of evaluation, I pulled out my pinched arm and studied Fred's sweaty brow as he stood awaiting my assessment.

"Well, Fred. There's a perfectly normal foal in there. Its head and feet are in a perfect position but I don't think she's in labor, yet." Fred stood there in amazement, knowing he had seen her lying down, and was certain she was straining as if in labor.

"Tell you what. Let's go inside and have some coffee, and we'll come out in an hour to check her." We were greeted in the breezeway as the door clicked open.

"So, what does she have?" a giddy Betty gasped with excitement.

I calmly said, "I don't believe that little guy wants to come out just yet, but everything feels fine inside. The foal is well positioned, so we'll just give it a little time and recheck her in about an hour." I pulled off my boots and took my usual place on the stool at the island counter. Intentionally changing the subject, I steered the conversation toward travel plans and family events.

Around midnight, after tromping through what remained of the crusted late spring snow, I looked at Star for the second and then third time for the night. There was no way that she was in labor. I convinced Fred that he should check in on Star every hour through the rest of the night. I would curl up on the soft leather couch by the Hoffman' fireplace and stay there until I was needed.

The aroma of frying bacon wafting through the house awakened me. This could have been a dream, but the horsey smell on my shirt sleeve rousted me to reality. "That was a short night," I cheerfully greeted the couple in the kitchen. They both looked sleep deprived and didn't quite share my rested opinion of the morning's arrival.

Three weeks later, deep into the night, the phone rang, rousing me to attention. "Good morning, this is Dr. Kenyon. How may I help you?"

It was Betty Hoffman this time who excitedly yelled, "It's coming for sure this time, and we'll meet you in the barn!" Click! I wanted to respond, but the click caught me in mid-sentence. I rolled back over, pulling the covers back over my chilled arm and shoulder. This move was always followed by my dear, now awakened, wife Cynthia's questioning.

"Who was that, and what did they want?" she emphatically asked.

"Oh, it was just Hoffmans again. Sounds like the foal is on its way finally," I groggily mumbled.

"Well...aren't you going?" She demanded.

"Cynthia," I groaned, "that foal will be out before I ever get there. I'll see it in the morning."

"You will not! They need you now! What if something goes wrong?" she continued her sermon as she put her cold feet in the middle of my back, pushing me out of bed.

I crawled out of my warm retreat, pulled on my clothes, grabbed a stocking hat and was out the door in minutes. On arrival at the scene of the action, I was greeted by all three Hoffmans beaming with excitement. Just as I had anticipated, the foal had indeed arrived and was wiggling in the straw with its mother smelling the little look-alike creature. The steam arose off the warm little arrival as the glistening placental membrane was removed from the rest of its body. The umbilical cord was cut, tied into a knot and disinfected with strong tincture of iodine. Its newborn head and neck bobbled, trying to adjust to the chill in the air. This was an abrupt change from the warm toasty womb!

I checked the placental covering, making sure it had all come out with the delivery. The butterfly shaped sac indicated that both horns of the uterus attachments had come out perfectly. The place where the foal had poked through with its feet and nose was found, and the full membrane was laid out on the straw. It was all there. I lifted a back leg to announce, "Star is the proud mother of a baby boy!".

The coaching, the night on the couch, and now this wobbly legged baby had fulfilled Laurie's dream. She had witnessed it being born. Little girls and their horses; they have a special, special bond like no other.

This little Laurie would eventually marry and take Star to her new home in southern Iowa where some lucky veterinarian helped care for Star's many episodes. Laurie would herself have a daughter who doted and sat on Star's back as soon as she could walk. The trails were blazed with stories and antics of yet another little girl and her passionate love for a horse.

Star lived out her life in retirement as the cycle continued with another little girl leaving home to find college, a husband, and a new home. One evening, Laurie came home from work to find Star at the gate to her pasture. Laurie gave her some feed, but she would not eat. Laurie petted and talked to her and went into the house. She went back before bed to check on Star. Star whinnied, and Laurie talked to her and petted her for quite some time. Star reached over to touch her face with her nose. She nosed both arms and walked away into the darkness. Star died that night at thirty-seven years of age. Three generations of Hoffmans, the memories, and stories of a girl and her horse would last forever.

About the Author

James Kenyon is a veterinarian. He will forever be a farmer boy. His interaction with animals was learned at a young age, growing up on a grain and livestock farm in Western Kansas.

Kenyon had a busy large and small animal practice in Iowa for 35 years. He believed in "all creatures great and small".

His patients were not only animals but their owners, too. His passion for helping people and their animals led him to bring these stories to light. Humans and animals have an innate need for each other.

Iowa, ah Iowa. The land of the tall corn, wonderful beauty, and loving people.